FEMALES OF THE SPECIES

FEMALES OF THE SPECIES

Semonides on Women

HUGH LLOYD-JONES

with photographs by

Don Honeyman

of sculptures by

MARCELLE QUINTON

NOYES PRESS

The business of him that republishes an ancient book is, to correct what is corrupt, and to explain what is obscure.

Samuel Johnson

Proposals for Printing the Dramatic Works of William Shakespeare, 1756

Contents

Preface

In these days when the question of women's rights is the subject of debate, the reader may be curious about the earliest work of European literature to have women for its theme. The poem on women by Semonides of Amorgos has been neglected in English. It is an interesting document in the history of attitudes to women; it is equally relevant to the history of character-study; and it seems to me one of the most attractive, as it is one of the largest, remains of Greek archaic poetry that have come down to us. This book contains an essay on the poem, a text and English translation, and a commentary.

The poem starts with descriptions of ten women, each standing for a type of woman. Seven are made out of animals—sow, vixen, bitch, ass, ferret, mare, monkey; two out of elements—earth and sea; and one out of a bee; all except the last are more or less unfavourably portrayed. That occupies the first ninety-three lines. Then the poet argues that women are the greatest curse that Zeus has sent to men. If a woman seems useful, that makes her all the more dangerous; it is hard for a married man to live happily or to escape poverty. If a husband tries to entertain a visitor, his wife finds a pretext for scolding and arms herself for battle. The wife who seems most respectable is the one who will soonest deceive her husband; and each husband blames everybody else's wife, but praises his own. Yes, women are the greatest curse; and now the poet embarks on a series of stories from myth designed to prove it. Soon after the beginning of this, the poem breaks off.

The poem appears in all the standard collections; but it has seldom had separate attention in English, and it has been given no separate English commentary. Nor has it made much impact upon English literature. The one striking exception is Joseph Addison's treatment in 1711, which is reproduced and discussed in an appendix to this book.

Most of the scholarly work devoted to the poem has been by Germans or in German. Two living scholars, Walter Marg and W. J. Verdenius, have written admirable commentaries; and Martin West in his edition of the Greek iambic and elegiac poets has published an excellent edition of the text.[1] I am greatly indebted

---

[1] See now West's *Studies in Greek Elegy and Iambus*, 1974.

Preface

to these three scholars, and Professor Marg has increased my obligation by allowing me an early view of a new article. I am grateful to my Oxford colleague Professor Martin Robertson for having kindly allowed me to print his excellent translation of the remarkable fragment of Archilochus lately published by Reinhold Merkelbach and Martin West.

Those who like to use the remains of early poetry to write the intellectual history (in German, *Geistesgeschichte*) of its time have tended to consider the tirade as a considered statement of its author's views upon its subject. The genre to which the poem belongs and the style in which it is written seem to me to make this way of approaching it a little dangerous. Its author's main purpose appears to have been to entertain his readers.

The book owes a special debt to its illustrator, to whose enthusiasm for Semonides—first acquired in the Bryn Mawr class of Richmond Lattimore, the author of the best English verse translation of the poem—it owes its origin.

Christ Church, Oxford   HUGH LLOYD-JONES
27 February, 1974

Introduction

1. *Iambic Poetry*

The Homeric poems are the product of a tradition that must have continued over many centuries; they are thought to have reached their final form during the eighth century before Christ.[1] During the same century[2] Hesiod wrote his account of the Greek gods, the *Theogony*, and also his didactic epic about farming, the *Works and Days*; the metre of both poems is the dactylic hexameter that was the traditional metre of epic poetry.

We have no poetry in other metres dating from before the seventh century. From that period we have fragments of the choral lyric of Alcman, perhaps a Lydian but resident at Sparta; and we have songs written for individual performance by Archilochus, a native of Paros but active in the colonisation of the rich island of Thasos. Some of these are written in the elegiac couplet, a dactylic metre closely connected with the hexameter; but others are written in a very different metre, the iambic trimeter, and others still are written in 'epodic' metres which are a mixture of dactylic and iambic metres.

Ancient writers liked to name an 'inventor' for each literary genre;[3] but when they tell us that Semonides or Archilochus 'invented' the poem called the iambus and the iambic metre, we do not have to take them seriously.[4] Evidence assembled from the history of many different cultures indicates that in most of them, if not all, song existed at a very early date.[5] We have a Greek specimen of songs sung at

---

[1] See *The Making of Homeric Verse: The Collected Papers of Milman Parry,* edited by Adam Parry, 1971; G. S. Kirk, *The Songs of Homer,* 1962, 282 f.

[2] See M. L. West, *Hesiod: Theogony,* 1966, 40 f.

[3] See A. Kleingünther, *Philologus* suppl. xxvi, heft 1, 1933.

[4] Pseudo-Plutarch, *De Musica* 28 (1141A) does this; he is believed by A. M. Dale, *Collected Papers,* 1969, 174–5.

[5] See the specimens of the poetry of peoples whose condition is thought to approximate to the primitive given by C. M. Bowra, *Primitive Song,* 1962 and K. J. Dover, 'The Poetry of Archilochos', *Archiloque: Entretiens de la Fondation Hardt* 10, 1964, 200 f.

work by grinders at the mill.[6] This cannot be very early, for it mentions Pittacus of Lesbos, who lived at the end of the seventh century; but songs of its type must have existed many centuries before. It simply happens that no such songs dating from before the seventh century have been preserved.

That some seventh-century songs were preserved is due to the greatness of poets like Alcman and Archilochus, whose poems seemed so memorable that they were written down and transmitted to posterity. But did great poets like these write songs, and not epics, because a new growth of individualism had compelled them to choose a medium suited to the expression of their individual feelings? So we are often told, on insufficient evidence. The remains of ancient epic do not suggest a world in which individualism was at a discount. True, the personality of the epic poet was not obtruded; but when we consider the nature of the genre, that hardly seems surprising. The personality of an iambic poet, like Archilochus, on the other hand, at first glance seems everywhere in evidence. Again, when we consider the nature of the genre we have to reconsider that impression.

In many of Archilochus' poems the poet was not at all times the speaker; he might put words into the mouths of other characters. The famous lines that begin 'I do not care for Gyges with all his gold'[7] were spoken not by the poet but by a carpenter called Charon; and the recently published fragments have supplied additional proof that the speech of other characters is so often rendered that it is not safe to assume that the sentiments expressed in an isolated scrap of Archilochian verse are those of Archilochus himself.[8]

Yet a number of Archilochus' poems are obviously the utterance of the poet. Often they are addressed to friends of his, like Pericles or that Glaucus whose actual tombstone has been found on Thasos;[9] often they deal with events of the poet's life, such as the wars in which he fought or his ill-starred connection with the daughters of Lycambes. Here we seem to catch the personal accent of a highly individual voice.

But even here, caution is necessary. A song written for a particular occasion

[6] Page *PMG* fr. 869; on such songs in general, see K. Bücher, *Arbeit und Rhythmus*, 6th edn., 1924. The hymn to Dionysus sung by the women of Elis (Page *PMG* fr. 871) may be very ancient.

[7] Fr. 19 West.

[8] See Dover, loc. cit., 208 f.

[9] See R. Meiggs and D. M. Lewis, *Greek Historical Inscriptions*, 1969, 3 f.; cf. J. Pouilloux, *Archiloque: Entretiens de la Fondation Hardt* 10, 1964, 14 f.

Introduction

reflects the mood of that occasion; it will express the sentiments appropriate to that mood. Even when these sentiments are those sincerely held by the poet, a point we do not always have the opportunity of verifying, they may well fail to accord with other sentiments expressed, perhaps with equal sincerity, on a different occasion. Archilochus' poems, like all Greek poems of the period, contain much reflection about the life of men and its relation to the gods. This reflection is never irrelevant to its context, and much of the poetry that contains it is great poetry. But comparison with other authors shows that the outlook which it expresses is one common to most Greeks at that time and for long afterwards. Although we still have very little of Archilochus, we can get some notion of his greatness as a literary artist. About his biography and about his personality we know less than our predecessors, with less material, imagined that they knew fifty years ago.[10]

The iambus was in iambic metre, either the trimeter or the tetrameter. Like the song in lyric metre, it was recited at the symposium, the drinking-party. The conventions of the occasion cannot have been without effect upon the conventions of the poems sung on it. Lyric or elegiac songs were accompanied on a musical instrument; iambics seem to have been delivered in recitative, *paracatalogê*.[11]

Elegiac and iambic poems are not as different in style and diction as has sometimes been imagined; Dover's careful examination has shown that the iambic poems owe hardly less to epic style and vocabulary than the elegiac. Yet I cannot accept that for Archilochus there was no generic difference between elegy and iambus; the latter uses words and mentions things which would not be appropriate to the more elevated poetical atmosphere in which the former moves. Elegy is used for a lament for dead friends, as in the poem to Pericles (fr. 13); the iambus is the place for the obscenities of frs. 40; 42; 43; 82, 4; 119; 252. Frs. 178 and 187 come, no doubt, from epodic poems; it may be significant that they come from iambic and not from dactylic portions. The iambus can rise to high poetry, as in 94, 105, 108, 120, 128; but it can also find a place for words and actions which no early writer mentions in elegiac verse. That is certainly true not only of the iambus of Archilochus, but of that of Semonides. The word ἴαμβος was connected with the

---

[10] But see Appendix III.

[11] Used by Archilochus, according to Pseudo-Plutarch, *De Musica* 28 (1141A); on this term, see Franca Perusino, *Quaderni Urbinati di Cultura Classica* 1, 1966, 9 f.

word ἰάπτω meaning 'to hurl'; it had the connotation of 'pelting with abuse'. The three iambic poets of the canon, Archilochus, Hipponax and Semonides, were all famous for abuse; according to Lucian,[12] each had a particular favourite victim. That of Archilochus was Lycambes, who was said to have promised the poet first one and then the other of his daughters and then broken his promise. Hipponax of Ephesus (about 600) attacked a sculptor called Bupalus, who had caricatured in a statue his notorious deformity. Lucian says that Semonides too had his special victim in one Orodoecides;[13] the suffix is Greek, but if the name is rightly transmitted, it must be of Oriental origin. None of the remains of his poetry which we possess seems to give evidence for personal abuse of any individual. But we have only forty-two fragments, only two of which are more than three lines long; and the tone of the longest and most celebrated piece among them certainly suggests an expert in invective. The other long fragment (fr. 1, twenty-four lines long)[14] contains, like several iambic poems of Archilochus, reflection about life of a comparatively elevated sort, which might easily have found expression in elegiac verse; so do several other fragments (2, 3, 4, for example). But others, though they contain no actual obscenities, seem to mention several things not likely to be treated in elegiac verse; they are about everyday birds and animals, or about food and cooking.[15] On the whole, then, the subject-matter seems to be like that of the Archilochian iambus.

Aristotle[16] remarked that the iambic metre was the one most suited to ordinary speech; it was made use of by the Athenian dramatists for the spoken portions of their plays. The Hellenistic Greeks called it 'pedestrian',[17] in comparison with the more elevated hexameter and lyric metres. It is not surprising that poems written in it should allow the mention of things considered below the dignity of more elevated verse.[17a]

---

[12] *Pseudologista* 2 (cited by West, *Iambi et Elegi Graeci* II, 97).

[13] West (l.c.) observes that the name does not even suit Semonides' metre; but if he had wanted to attack someone called that, I think he would have contrived to do so by means of the licence poets often allowed themselves when proper names were in question.

[14] See Appendix I.

[15] The principles found at work in Latin poetry by Bertil Axelson in his *Unpoetische Wörter* (1945) are not without relevance to Greek also.

[16] *Poetics* 4, 1449a24 f.; cf. *Rhet.* 3, 8, 1408b33 f.

[17] See Pfeiffer on Callimachus, fr. 112, 9.

[17a] On the iambus and the iambic metre, see now West, *Studies in Greek Elegy and Iambus*, 1974, 22 f.

Introduction

2. *Semonides of Amorgos*

Semonides of Amorgos is an obscure figure. His date is known only vaguely, and his life hardly at all; even the correct form of his name is uncertain. Almost all writers who mention him call him 'Simonides'.[18] But an ancient grammarian asserts explicitly that his name was written with an 'e';[19] and the danger of confusion with the better-known Simonides of Ceos, who lived from 556 to 468, makes it expedient to believe him. Simonides of Ceos is not known to have written iambics, and of the iambic verses quoted under this name all, or almost all, have the air of belonging to an earlier poet. Only in one case is there serious doubt as to which of the two poets a poem belongs to, and that is an elegiac poem.[20]

Amorgos[21] is one of the Sporades, a small island lying south-east of Naxos and north-west of Astypalaea. It is quite long, but very narrow; most of it consists of high mountains, and only the north-west coast is flat enough to be inhabited. Settlers from Naxos came first, and founded the harbour town of Arcesine and perhaps that of Aegialus or Aegiale also; later came another party, from Samos, and they resettled these places and founded a new harbour called Minoa. If we can accept the probable guess that part of the article on Semonides in the Byzantine encyclopaedia called the Suda has become mixed up with the article on the much later Rhodian poet Simmias, the poet Semonides came to Amorgos as the leader of these Samian settlers.[22]

[18] See P. Maas, *R.–E.* s.v., 1929, 184.

[19] Choeroboscus in *Et. Magn.* 713, 17c. Choeroboscus lived in the sixth century A.D. (see R. Reitzenstein, *Geschichte der griechischen Etymologika*, 1897, 190, n. 4).

[20] See Appendix I.

[21] See Hirschfeld in *R.–E.* I, 1893, 1875–6; L. Ross, *Reise auf den griechischen Inseln* I, 1840, 173 f.; A. Miliarakis, *Amorgos*, 1884; H. Hauttecoeur, 'L'isle d'Amorgos', *Soc. Roy. Belge de Géographie, Bulletin* 23, 1899, 90 f., 145 f.; A. Philippson and E. Kirsten, *Griechische Landschaften* 4, 148 f.

[22] Suda iv 360, 7 (cited by West, *IEG* II p. 96). It used to be held that Amorgos remained a dependency of Samos until the time of the Athenian Empire, but this is doubtful (see F. A. Lepper, *Journal of Hellenic Studies* 82, 1962, 41). That part of an article about Semonides has found its way into the article about Simmias was first seen by G. J. Vossius (d. 1649) (see his *Opera* III, 201), not by Bernhardy in his edition of the Suda, as was supposed by J. A. Davison, *Eranos* 53, 130, n. 1. Davison seems to doubt whether the guess is right; he seems not to know Stephanus of Byzantium p. 86, 9f., which is omitted from the testimonia given by J. M. Edmonds, *Elegy and Iambus* II, 1931, 210, and which confirms Vossius' view.

The colonisation is presumed to have happened at some time during the seventh century.[23] That suits the dates given for Semonides. The Suda places him 490 years after the Trojan War; since that was conventionally dated in 1170, that puts him in 680.[24] Cyril of Alexandria gives his date as 640.[25] Proclus[26]—probably not the Neoplatonist of the fifth century after Christ, but a grammarian of the second—makes him contemporary with Ananius of Macedonia. There was no such person, and the name must be corrupt. If it is corrupt for that of the Macedonian king Amyntas, it would indicate a sixth-century date; but if it is corrupt for the earlier king Argaeus, it would point to a date between 640 and 610, and so harmonise with the other evidence. Some have connected the colonisation with the fall of a Samian tyrant Demoteles, thought to have happened about 600.[27] But that is only a guess, and we have no way of dating Semonides precisely. Archilochus was certainly active during the middle of the seventh century; the eclipse of the sun which he witnessed was that of 6 April, 648 B.C.[28] Some ancient writers take him and some take Semonides to be the earlier; Clement[29] says that their careers overlapped.

We know almost nothing of Samian domestic history during the seventh century, but we know something of Samian activities overseas. At this time Samos had trading links with Al Mina in Syria, with the Hellespontine area and with Egypt; about 630 a Samian ship made its way to Spain.[30] In the Lelantine War over the rich Lelantine plain in Euboea Samos fought on the side of Chalcis

[23] G. Busolt, *Griechische Geschichte* I, 2nd edn., 1893, 300–1; cf. W. Ruppel, *Klio* 21, 1927, 313 f.

[24] Davison, art. cit. in note 22, p. 131, thinks the date given is 780; he has followed Edmonds in giving the figure to mean '390 years after the Trojan War', whereas it is actually '490 years'. It is a pity that we still have to use Edmonds' *Lyra Graeca* and *Elegy and Iambus* for their testimonia, for these are as incomplete and as inaccurate as the treatment of the actual texts in these books would lead one to expect.

[25] *Contra Iulianum* I, 12.

[26] Proclus ap. Phot. Bibl. Cod. 239, 319B30 Bekker = 31, p. 40 in A. Severyns, *Recherches sur la Chréstomathie de Procle* I, 1937.

[27] On Demoteles see J. P. Barron, *Class. Quart.* 14, 1964, 211.

[28] See F. Jacoby, *Class. Quart.* 35, 1941, 97 f.

[29] *Strom.* I 21 (I p. 82,2 Stählin).

[30] Al Mina: see G. L. Huxley, *The Early Ionians*, 1966, 64; J. Boardman, *The Greeks Overseas*², 1973, 46. The Hellespontine area: Huxley, l.c.; Boardman, op. cit., 235. Egypt: Huxley, op. cit., 74; Boardman, op. cit., 131, 140 f.; M. M. Austin, 'Greece and Egypt in the Archaic Age', *Proc. Cam. Phil. Soc. Suppl.* 2, 1970, 9; etc.

against Eretria and her own neighbour and rival Miletus, and finished on the winning side; during the Messenian revolt that began about 640, she sent help to Sparta. We know more of Samos during the sixth century, the most notable in her history. The great tyrant Polycrates built the famous temple of Hera, the tunnel through Mount Ampelus and the harbour wall. He was the patron of the poets Ibycus and Anacreon and of the famous school of Samian sculptors. Under his rule, the Samian fleet for a brief moment held the balance of naval power between Persia and the Egypt of Amasis. About this time flourished the most celebrated of all Samians, the mysterious Pythagoras.[31] Even during the seventh century Samos must have been one of the most energetic of the Greek communities, and one of those with the widest foreign contacts.

Some have thought the story of Semonides' leadership of the colony to be a fabrication, made to harmonise his career with that of Archilochus, who took part in the Parian colonisation of Thasos. This seems unlikely; fabrications were not made simply for the sake of symmetry. The story may well have come from some early Samian chronicler; one such writer, Euagon, or whatever the right form of his name was, lived before the Peloponnesian War.[32]

Semonides himself may have written a work of a historical character. The notice under his name in the Suda says that besides iambi he wrote an elegy in two books.[33] Perhaps the number two really belongs to the books into which the iambi were arranged; a second book of the iambi is twice quoted.[34] But another notice in the Suda, the one that has become confused with the notice on the poet Simmias,[35] says that besides iambi and 'various things' he wrote 'an archaeology of the Samians'. That title cannot be as old as Semonides; but he may well have written a poem about Samian history. The guess that equates it with the elegy may possibly be right. A later Samian poet, Asius, wrote during the fifth century[36] an elegiac poem which mentioned at least one detail about early Samian customs.

---

[31] For his life, see W. Burkert, *Lore and Science in Ancient Pythagoreanism*, 1972.

[32] Euagon is no. 535 in *FGH*; see the commentary there; cf. Jacoby, *Klio* 9, 1909, 115, 120 = *Abhandlungen zur griechischen Geschichtsschreibung*, 1956, 54, 60; K. von Fritz, *Die griechische Geschichtsschreibung* I ii, 1967, 54, n. 4.

[33] Suda iv 363, 1 (cited by West, *IEG* ii, 96).

[34] West, op. cit., 97, gives the quotations.

[35] Quoted in n. 22 above.

[36] See C. M. Bowra, *Hermes* 85, 1957, 391 f. = *In Greek Margins*, 1970, 122 f.

Jacoby[37] thought that Semonides might have written a poem about the colonisation of Amorgos in which he himself had taken part.

3. *Hesiod*

It is obvious that the poem is influenced by one Greek writer earlier than Semonides—Hesiod of Ascra in Boeotia, who is usually thought to have written during the eighth century. He twice tells the story of the making of the first woman. In his *Theogony*[38] he tells how Prometheus tricked Zeus into choosing for himself the inferior instead of the superior share of the meat of the sacrificial victim. Zeus retaliates by depriving men, Prometheus' protégés, of fire, and Prometheus steals fire from heaven in order to restore it to them. Then to be revenged Zeus tells Hephaestus to mould a woman from earth and together with Athene to adorn her. Her appearance excites the admiration both of gods and men; but she proves a disaster to the latter, because from her descends the race of women, a great plague to mortals when they live with men, adapted not to deadly poverty, but to pride. Women, conspirators in evil works, are like the drones which sit uselessly at home while the working bees are out collecting food. Another curse which Zeus lays upon men is that anyone who chooses to remain a bachelor can protect his property, but only at the price of having no children to look after him when he is old and to inherit his possessions. The man who marries a good and sensible wife acquires good mixed with evil; the man who marries a bad one lives in utter misery.

In his later poem, the *Works and Days*,[39] Hesiod offers a somewhat different version of the myth. While urging his brother Perses to work hard for a living instead of trying to cheat him, he explains how Zeus came to ordain that men must work. Prometheus stole fire to give to men, and Zeus then warned him that in return for this he would send men a curse in which they would all delight, embracing their own ruin. With a loud laugh Zeus ordered Hephaestus to make the woman out of earth and water, Athene to teach her weaving, Aphrodite to invest her with beauty, but also with dangerous desirability and the power to cause torments that gnaw the limbs, and Hermes to give her a bitch's mind and thievish

[37] See *FGH* IIIb, Kommentar zu 297–607, 1955, 456.
[38] 510 f.　See J. P. Vernant, *Mythe et société en Grèce ancienne*, 1974, 177 f.
[39] 42 f.

habits. Hermes gives her crafty speech and thievish habits as Zeus commands, and then endows her with a voice and calls her Pandora, because she has been given gifts by all the gods.

Hermes now took her to Epimetheus, whose name means 'Afterthinker', a brother of Prometheus, 'the Forethinker'. His brother had warned him to accept no gift from Zeus, for fear it proves a curse in disguise; but Epimetheus only recognised the disaster when he had it. Formerly human beings lived on the earth removed from troubles and hateful pain and dread diseases, which give the fates of death to men; but now the woman removed the lid of a great jar and scattered them abroad, and caused mournful sorrows for mankind. Hope alone remained inside the jar, and did not fly out before the woman replaced the lid. Many other plagues wander among men, for earth and sea alike are full of evils, and diseases come of their own accord, some by day and some by night, silently, because Zeus has taken away their voice.

In the *Works and Days* the woman releases plagues by opening the jar; in the earlier account, she is herself the curse which Zeus sends to mortals. Neither account is at all flattering to women; and the attitude towards them adopted in the practical suggestions offered later in the poem, though not downright hostile, is both utilitarian and defensive. The farmer must start by providing himself with a wife and an ox for ploughing.[40] 'At the proper season,' Hesiod tells his farmer,[41] 'bring a wife to your home, when you are not much less than thirty years old and not much more; that is the time for marriage. Let the woman be ripe for four years and marry in the fifth. Marry a virgin, so that you can teach her good habits; and marry her who lives closest to you, surveying everything about her cautiously, so that you do not turn out to have married for the neighbours' pleasure. A man gets nothing better than a good woman and nothing more horrid than a bad one, one who guzzles dainties, who needs no torch to singe her husband, however stout a fellow he may be, and gives him to cruel old age.'

The *Theogony* myth, in which the woman is herself the plague, is more germane to Semonides than the *Works and Days* myth, in which she brings disaster upon man by opening the jar. The *Theogony* myth stresses the extravagance and uselessness of women; the other myth mentions their cunning and their thievish propensities. The references to women that come later in the *Works and Days*

---

[40] 405.   [41] 695 f.

strike a rather different note from that of the myth. The poet is particularly afraid of woman's greed and extravagance. But he allows that if married young and carefully trained she may acquire good habits, and actually concedes that though there is nothing worse than a bad wife there is nothing better than a good one, a sentiment repeated, with a clear echo of Hesiod, in a fragment of Semonides that does not form part of the iambus about women.[41A] We need not be troubled by the apparent inconsistency between the complete condemnation of women in the myth of the *Works and Days* and the qualified condemnation of the later part of the poem. We should expect the myth of woman's origin to represent her as a plague, but the practical suggestions about farming life to make some modification of this judgment.

Hesiod was certainly known to Semonides; the commentary will indicate some verbal echoes.[42] Yet the myth of woman's creation used by Semonides is not the same as either of Hesiod's versions of the story of Pandora. The legend that different women were made out of different animals is very unlikely to have been Semonides' own invention.[43] Various similar myths attested from comparatively modern times might, it is true, have been influenced by the Semonidean story, or have come into existence independently.[44] But the story has all the characteristics of a folktale. Four of the Semonidean types of woman—bitch, bee, sow and mare—occur in the gnomic elegiac verses of Phocylides,[45] a writer not easy to date but belonging to the sixth or, more probably, the fifth century; despite some similarity of language, we are not forced to believe that he knew the legend from Semonides. Other similar stories are known from other poets. The Hellenistic

[41A] Fr. 6.

[42] The apparent echo of *Op.* 702–3 in Semonides fr. 6 has often been noted; see p. 92 below.

[43] 'Fabula fuit popularis, ut videtur, et fortasse ultimae antiquitatis, quam a Simonide inventam esse, idcirco, quia apud antiquiorem scriptorem illius non fit mentio, quae vulgaris est argumentandi ratio, non est temere statuendum': Welcker, *Rh. Mus.* 3, 1835, 386; cf. J. T. Kakridis, *Krêtika Chronika* 15/16, 1963, 294 f. = *Meletes kai Arthra*, 1971, 24 f. (in modern Greek; German version in *Wiener Humanistische Blätter* 5, 1962, 1 f.).

[44] This is the view of Kakridis; but caution is needed. Those who are interested in finding survivals of ancient Greek myths in modern Greek folktales should study carefully the article in *Rh. Mus.* 115, 1972, 173, in which D. Fehling has exposed to critical scrutiny the opinion, held by R. M. Dawkins and recently approved by so critical a scholar as P. M. Fraser (*Ptolemaic Alexandria* II, 1972, 916–17), that a Coan folktale derives from the myth of Erysichthon narrated by Callimachus in his sixth hymn.

[45] Fr. 2 Diehl: see Appendix II. On his date, see West *SGEI*, 65 f.

poet Callimachus[46] is not likely to have made up the story that different men were given the voices of different animals; he will have taken it from a folktale to use it for his own satirical purpose of ascribing the voices of various animals to particular contemporaries. Horace's[47] fable that man's irascibility was due to an element in his nature derived from the lion also seems ancient.

4. *The Beast Fable*

The legend has an obvious affinity with the beast fable. No kind of story has a longer history than this; it already existed in Egypt three thousand years before Christ. The Greeks ascribed their beast fables to Aesop, who according to legend was the Phrygian slave of Pythagoras, and so lived during the sixth century. The fables were not systematically collected and edited until Demetrius of Phalerum, at the end of the fourth century B.C. The Aesopic collection we possess is in its present form not earlier than the time of the Roman Empire. But the fables themselves must in many cases be far older than the sixth century, and we have evidence that some circulated in Oriental countries a good deal earlier than they are likely to have done in Greece.[48]

The legend most like that used by Semonides is an Aesopic fable[49] which says that Prometheus at first created too many animals and had not enough material left for men, so that he was forced to change some animals into men, and there are some men who have human exteriors but bestial souls. This may have been known to Semonides. It is possible that he adapted it so as to make the humans with bestial souls be women; but it is also possible that his account of the making of women was taken over ready-made from an existing folktale.

The beast fable had found its way into literature as early as Hesiod, who in the *Works and Days* (202 f.) had used the fable of the harmless nightingale in the claws of the ruthless hawk to drive home the helplessness of innocence against naked power. It had been used in memorable fashion by Archilochus, who in his

---

[46] Fr. 192 Pfeiffer.

[47] Horace, *Odes* I, 16, 9; see R. G. M. Nisbet and M. E. Hubbard, *A Commentary on Horace: Odes I*, 1970, 209.

[48] See M. L. West, *Harvard Studies in Classical Philology* 73, 1968, 113 f.

[49] 228 Hausrath = 383 Halm = 140 Perry.

epodes told the stories of the fox and the eagle and of the fox and the monkey to describe allegorically incidents of his own life.

5. *The Poem on Women*

The poem about women by Semonides of Amorgos is by far the longest specimen of the Greek literary genre known as the iambus that has been preserved. Its end is missing, and we cannot know for certain how much of it there originally was; but we possess 115 lines. Woman's mind was made separately by the god, the poet begins; and he goes on to describe nine disagreeable kinds of women, seven made from animals and two others from earth and sea. Only the tenth kind, made from a bee, makes a good wife; all the others are portrayed satirically. This occupies the first 93 lines of the poem; and the last 22 consist of general reflections upon women in which they are condemned wholesale, without even an exception in favour of the bee-woman.

Considering its historical interest as a specimen of early Greek poetry, as an early diatribe on the interesting subject of the female sex and as a document of some significance in the history of literary character-study, the poem has aroused little interest among scholars, at any rate in England; virtually all the important work done upon it has been done by Germans or in the German language. Most of those modern scholars who have discussed it have not valued it highly. It consists, Wilamowitz[50] thought, of crude mockery of women, pretty well without wit and lacking in charm of presentation. Bethe[51] called it 'dry, long-winded, lacking in wit, without appeal and without art'. Hermann Fränkel,[52] who thinks the poem is important as an example of archaic modes of thought, finds that its literary value is slight. Its tone has drawn down much disapproval upon its author. Ludwig Radermacher[53] thinks he was a man of crooked morals, though we must make allowances for him, because he led a hard life, and G. L. Huxley[54] remarks that 'the poet's stringent criticisms of women and rather pedestrian notions suggest that the Samian settlers may not have found his rule enlightened'.

[50] In the history of Greek literature in *Die Kultur der Gegenwart*², 1912 (1st edn., 1905).
[51] *Die griechische Dichtung*, 1927, 78.
[52] *Dichtung und Philosophie des frühen Griechentums*, 2nd edn., 1962, 236.
[53] *Weinen und Lachen*, 1947, 160.
[54] *The Early Ionians*, 1966, 64.

Introduction

When we have examined the poem more closely, we shall be able to enquire whether these estimates are deserved.

In judging any poem, it is important to bear in mind the literary genre it belongs to and its own place within it.[55] We have seen that the iambus may be the vehicle of more or less elevated reflections about life in general; so it is in the next longest fragment of Semonides (fr. 1), whose subject-matter is remarkably like that of an elegiac poem which may or may not belong to the same author (fr. 8).[56] But the iambus may be used for purposes that are less elevated; in particular, it may be used for satire. Addison described our poem, not unfairly in the language of his time, as a satire; it is not a satire on an individual, like many of the iambi of Archilochus, but a satire on an entire sex. Wilamowitz[57] pointed out that at certain Greek religious festivals, including the ceremonies which preceded the Eleusinian mysteries, women uttered abuse against men as part of the ritual. The abuse uttered by women during the procession to Eleusis was associated with the figure of the old woman who was supposed to have amused Demeter during the time of her sorrow by her ribaldries. This old woman was called Iambe; she was therefore the personification of the iambus and its spirit. Wilamowitz suggested that the iambus of Semonides was designed as a reply on behalf of men to the abuse of men uttered by women on these occasions. This seems to me improbable; the abuse spoken by women on religious occasions was part of a ritual, originating from an attempt to promote fertility, and could hardly have provoked an answer delivered on that or any other occasion. But the notion that the abuse of women was a regular literary theme, appropriate to the iambus and having conventions of its own, seems to have much in its favour. We find the motive in Hesiod, where it is handled in a somehow different tone, and we shall find it later in tragedy and comedy, again with a tone appropriate to the genre. Semonides' way of handling it seems highly characteristic of his own genre, that of the iambus.

---

[55] On the importance of literary genre in ancient literature, see L. E. Rossi, *Bulletin of the London Institute of Classical Studies* 18, 1971, 69 f. and in *Dialoghi di Archeologia*, anno 6, 2–3, 1972, 248–54; cf. F. Cairns, *Generic Composition in Greek and Roman Poetry*, 1972.

[56] See Appendix I.

[57] *Einleitung in die Attische Tragödie*, 1889, 57, n. 17 and again, *Der Glaube der Hellenen* I, 1931, 293, n. 1; cf. K. Latte, *GGA* 207, 1953, 37–8 = *Kleine Schriften*, 1968, 721; against, W. Marg, *Der Charakter in der Sprache der frühgriechischen Dichtung*, 2nd edn., 1962, 108.

Females of the Species

When we evaluate this poem, we must keep the nature of that genre under consideration. Fränkel[58] compares Semonides unfavourably with Hesiod; Hesiod, he says, is dignified and enlightened, and Semonides is not; Hesiod penetrates from the exterior of things to their inner nature, and everything in his poem stands in its context; his striking images always illustrate some counsel or some warning; Semonides is superficial in his thought, and slack in his presentation, and his imaginative power suffices only for details.

Fränkel denies that this difference is due to the difference of genre, pointing to the iambus of Archilochus, with its concentrated power and elegance of form. It is true that Archilochus is a great poet and Semonides is not. Yet in his poem about women Semonides is attempting something not aimed at in any of the surviving fragments of Archilochus, and comparison with Hesiod is not the fairest way of judging it.

Fränkel's failure to understand the poem's purpose is evident from his complaint that Semonides has allowed the combination of characteristics found in the animals to dictate that found in the women. The dirty and untidy woman, he says, has to be greedy too, because the pig is greedy; the obstinate woman has to be greedy, because the ass is greedy. Fränkel seems to assume that the poet's aim is to provide a systematic anatomy of female character; it seems not to have occurred to him that Semonides may wish to amuse his audience. The tirade against woman must have been not uncommon; the various specimens which appear in extant literature suggest that this was so. As Dover[59] has reminded us in connection with Archilochus, a song usually expresses a feeling or a mood. The iambus against women gives full expression to a jaundiced view of women of a standard type. We should be wary of taking it for granted that it represents the writer's personal attitude, or that it is intended as a serious study of the subject.

That the poem is intended to amuse does not, I trust, need demonstration. It has been remarked that it is written from the viewpoint of the peasant,[60] or at least of the ordinary man. In the archaic age people living on the Aegean islands lived close to nature, as they still do; the modern scholar who found it strange that in Aeschylus' *Diktyoulkoi*[61] the brother of the king of Seriphos seems to be a

[58] Quoted in n. 52 above.
[59] Quoted in n. 5 above.
[60] Thus Radermacher, op. cit., 158 and (at first) Marg, op. cit., 37–9; for Marg's second thoughts, see p. 108.
[61] See frs. 274–5 in my appendix to the Loeb edition.

fisherman had not considered the size of that island or the conditions of life upon it. At the same time, the likelihood that Semonides was the leader of the colony, and therefore an important man, should put us on our guard against assuming that the social environment in which the poem is located was necessarily his own; by the same reasoning, one might deduce that Petronius must have moved in the circles which the *Satyrica* depict.

6. *Women in Greek Literature*

So many scholars have taken the poem as a deliberate statement of its author's opinions about women that it is necessary to consider the subject of their treatment in Greek literature.[62] It is notorious that in Greece at this time and for a long time afterwards women suffered under many social and legal disabilities. They lacked political rights, even in fifth-century Athens. A woman had to have a legal guardian of the male sex, and though she could transmit property to males, she could not fully control what was her own without that guardian's consent. A wife was in the power of her husband, and divorce was not easy, at any rate without active help from her own family; even then, she might have to sacrifice her dowry. The penalties for adultery were severe; the institution of marriage was above all else an important element in the system under which property was held. All this applies even to fifth-century Athens; our knowledge of social life in seventh-century Ionia is most imperfect, but on the whole women living in this part of Greece, in close proximity to Oriental neighbours, enjoyed less liberty than women did in mainland Greece.

It is also well known that for many male persons in archaic Greece, particularly among members of the higher social classes, boys and young men rather than women were the chief object of erotic interest.[63] It is thought that this state of affairs was promoted by the women's unemancipated state and lack of proper education. Semonides' poem, like Hesiod's Pandora myths, is often quoted as an illustration of the contemptuous attitude to women promoted by the social and sexual disabilities from which they suffered.

It must of course be conceded that the women portrayed in the heroic epic do

---

[62] There is a balanced treatment of the subject, with good bibliography, in J. Vogt, 'Von der Gleichwertigkeit der Geschlechter in der bürgerlichen Gesellschaft der Griechen', *Abh. der Mainzer Akademie*, 1960, nr. 2.

[63] See, most recently, G. Devereux, *Symbolae Osloenses* 42, 1967, 69 f.

not accord with the picture of a depressed inferior sex. The portrayal of Andromache and Penelope shows that the writers of the *Iliad* and the *Odyssey* were well aware of the most favourable aspects under which married life may appear. The presentation of Helen in the *Iliad* shows the poet to be wholly aware of the power of such a woman, and the nature of her attraction is most subtly exhibited by her speech and her behaviour. In the *Odyssey* she is shown back at Sparta as if nothing had happened, in full command of household and husband and behaving with the same gentle modesty and distinguished courtesy that make her, in the earlier poem, so fascinating and so redoubtable. Women's position in the epic age, we are often told, is different. Even Semonides feels differently about the upper classes; disastrous as she is for a peasant, the mare-woman (l. 57 f.) makes a suitable wife for a king. But we must remember that Semonides' original audience certainly knew the epic, and the attitude to women found in it was one of those which they had to take into account. Nor is there anything about the married life of Hector and Andromache or of Odysseus and Penelope which is specifically royal or aristocratic.

Hesiod is indeed a serious writer, concerned to instruct his hearers in religion and in morals. The nature of the myths of the creation of woman which he recounts is certainly not without significance for the general attitudes towards them of Greek society; and the remarks about a wife's duty in the part of his poem that contains practical advice shows that in a poor man's household a wife was expected to manage the household economically and produce children. But we must make allowance for Hesiod's general tone. The government of the world by the gods is shown with a tough-minded realism; the practical advice to farmers is correspondingly hard-headed. On the metaphysical plane, so to speak, represented by the creation myth, Hesiod holds that it is a pity man cannot reproduce his species without woman's help; on the practical plane represented by the later part of the poem, he is willing to allow that some good wives can be found. He is not concerned, as Semonides is, to exploit the comic possibilities of the wives who are less good. Hesiod is another poet whom Semonides' audiences will have known; his attitude to women was doubtless close to their own. But it is not identical with that found in Semonides' poem, and the difference may at least partly be accounted for by the difference of literary purpose.

Other considerations should warn us against generalisations based too exclusively upon the disapproval of women expressed in Hesiod and Semonides. In

Introduction

eastern Greece itself, less, and perhaps much less, than a century after Semonides, we find Sappho and the society in which she moved. Mysterious as that society is, it can hardly be doubted that Sappho was, by the standards of the time, well educated—she knew the poets well—and that she and other women known to her enjoyed a certain degree of personal freedom. Sappho was of course an aristocrat, like Cimon's sister Elpinice[64] and Pericles' mistress Aspasia. Women with husbands of some means certainly enjoyed considerable power in their own households; that is clear even from the condescending lectures to his wife given by Xenophon's priggish young Athenian, Ischomachus.[65] Women in a lower social class naturally had fewer opportunities; they will have had to work hard at domestic duties, as Hesiod and Semonides indicate. But it is matter for simple observation that in those modern countries by the Mediterranean where women are in theory unemancipated in comparison with those in England or America, many women know how to get their way in dealings with men just as well as, if not better than, their supposedly freer counterparts; and we have good grounds for thinking that this was true in antiquity also. The housewife of Greek comedy, both old and new, can hold her own. She may be an aristocratic spendthrift, like the wife of Strepsiades;[66] she may be a nagging scold, especially if, like Crobyle in Menander's *Plokion*[67] or Nausistrata in the Apollodoran original of Terence's *Phormio*, she is a rich heiress. Again, just as the prevalence of arranged marriages in modern France does not mean that romantic sentiment towards women does not exist, comedy proves unmistakably that many Athenians did fall in love with women. Nor must this love in every case be written off as crude desire; the young husbands in Menander's *Epitrepontes*, Apollodorus' *Hecyra* and the prologue of a lost play, perhaps by Menander,[68] are as genuinely attached to their wives as is the husband of Semonides' bee-woman.

In Aristophanic comedy women have a sense of forming, for certain purposes, a kind of separate community. At their own secret festival, they plan revenge on

[64] An ostrakon used to record a vote during an ostracism which has lately been found at Athens is inscribed, 'Let Cimon go and take Elpinice with him', D. M. Lewis tells me.

[65] Xenophon, *Oeconomicus* vi, 17 f.

[66] See Aristophanes, *Nub.* 46 f.

[67] See in particular frs. 333–4 Koerte-Thierfelder (on pp. 311–13 of F. H. Sandbach's Oxford text of Menander).

[68] Speaking of his wife he says (P. Antinoop. 15, 11–12): 'Won by her generous nature and unaffected manner, I became fond of my loving wife.' See p. 85 below.

Euripides; they organise a sexual strike under the dignified priestess Lysistrata; they take over the Assembly and introduce communism under the formidable housewife Praxagora. To Aristophanes and his audience, the very idea of women taking part in such activities is irresistibly funny; such events as these belong to the comic world of fantasy. At the same time, it is significant that such fantasies existed. The fantasy of the women's assembly has an obvious relationship to the views about communism and women's liberation actually expressed by Plato but in circulation, as Aristophanes' play shows, long before his time.[69] Even in the *Oresteia*, produced in 458 B.C., the clash between man and woman forms one of the trilogy's pervading themes;[70] man's essential superiority is upheld, but the fact that man and woman and their respective claims are pitted against each other is significant. Creon in the *Antigone* strongly objects to being defied by a woman; Creon is a personage whose actions do not command approval.[71] In pity for Medea at her desertion by Jason, the chorus of Euripides' *Medea* (431) sing a great ode of defiance against men; 'honour,' they declare, 'is coming to the race of women; no longer shall evil repute be ours.'[72] Beyond any question, in the age of the great sophists the question of women's rights was in the air. To understand the significance of this, one must remember that nothing of the kind had occurred, to the best of our knowledge, in any of the surrounding civilisations at the time in question. In respect of women's liberties, as in so many other ways, the Greeks must be admitted to have been pioneers.

The basic Greek attitude to women was, like the basic Greek attitude to most permanent features of human life, realistic and disillusioned. It finds expression in Hesiod's myths about Pandora; it is exploited, for a purpose that is above all comic, in Semonides' poem. But in the practical advice given by Hesiod and in Semonides' account of his bee-woman, we find these authors reluctant to generalise in practice from the wholesale condemnation that their metaphysic would demand; and that reluctance seems typical of men's attitude over a long period. It

---

[69] The question has been recently discussed by R. G. Ussher on p. xvi f. of his commentary on the *Ecclesiazusae* (1973). For an excellent treatment of the subject of women in Aristophanes, see the references to them in the index of K. J. Dover's *Aristophanic Comedy* (1972).

[70] See R. P. Winnington-Ingram, 'Clytemnestra and the Vote of Athena', *Journal of Hellenic Studies* 68, 1948, 130 f.

[71] Sophocles, *Ant.* 484–5; 525; 678; 740; 746; 756.

[72] E., *Med.* 419–20. This chorus in Gilbert Murray's translation was chanted by suffragettes in the streets of London.

is significant that this culture was by a long way the first to give serious consideration to the question of whether the subordination of women which had from time immemorial been a fact of life was or was not unjust. Surely we should be wary of reading Semonides' poem as though it were the serious and deliberate pronouncement of a writer for whom truth came first and entertainment only second.[72A]

7. Character in Greek Literature

Semonides has a special place in the history of character-study; he may be considered an ancestor of Theophrastus[73] and through him of the whole tradition that includes La Bruyère in France and Overbury and Earle in England. Modern historians of ideas have explained to us that his notion of character is primitive. Snell[74] complains that 'the types (of women) are rigidly fixed according to the animal from which each one of them is descended'; he is following Fränkel,[75] who finds fault with Semonides for making some characteristics belong to several different types of woman simply because he was not capable of thinking of enough different qualities to supply ten different kinds of female nature. He blames him for allowing the types of woman to be fixed by the types of animal; the sluttish woman and the stubborn woman both have to be greedy, because the pig and ass both are.

The whole point of Semonides' poem is that certain types of women do resemble certain animals; perhaps the same is true of certain types of men, but that is not relevant. The types which he sketches very naturally have certain qualities in common; it would be surprising if any poet, however imaginative, could describe ten different types of women without a single common quality, and his description would hardly be very true to life. To complain that his types are not exhaustive of those that exist, or that a few of them combine qualities not regularly found together, would be to ignore the poet's real purpose. Any unbiased reader

---

[72A] Snell, op. cit., 279, n. 78, calls it 'a systematic survey of the possible women's characters'.

[73] The relation of Theophrastus' *Characters* to his philosophical works has been much debated; see O. Regenbogen in *R.–E.* suppl. vii, 1950, 1504 f., and O. Navarre in the introduction to his edition of 1920. G. Pasquali (*Rassegna Italiana di Lingue e Letterature Classiche* I ii, 1918, 73–9; iii, 143–50; II i, 1919, 1–21) suggested that they formed a kind of phenomenology of ethics akin to Book IV of the *Nicomachean Ethics*. In this work Theophrastus is an artist as well as a philosopher; his sharp and malicious observation has obvious affinities with comedy.

[74] *Poetry and Society*, 1961, 78.

[75] Op. cit. in n. 52 above, 235.

will admit that on the whole the types of women that Semonides describes have enough verisimilitude to be amusing; and if their qualities did not correspond with those of the animals in question, the point of the joke would vanish. We shall understand and enjoy the poem best if we approach it not as a metaphysical or sociological treatise, but as a work of art of its particular kind intended to give entertainment.

The notion that the Greeks of Semonides' time were capable only of a primitive conception of human character cannot, I think, be justified. Semonides and his contemporaries were familiar with the Homeric epic, whose characterisation, if its aims and methods are properly understood, is of unusual strength and subtlety. In Greek literature the main concern is the action, and the actors must be characterised so far as to appear capable of the actions credited to them by the story.[76] To a great degree the authors are indifferent to personal idiosyncrasy and delicate psychological shading; and the generations that brought the exploration of character to the pitch it reached in the work of Joyce, Proust and their contemporaries were apt either to read into Greek literature nuances of characterisation that were not really there or else to write it off as demonstrably defective in this important literary skill. For examples of the former tendency, we need look no further than the unconvincing psychological explanations of the actions of characters in Greek tragedy that were in general currency before Tycho von Wilamowitz'[77] celebrated study of Sophoclean dramatic technique began to have effect. Examples of the second tendency are furnished by works influenced by the theory of the gradual linear development of Greek intellectual concepts whose best-known exponent is Bruno Snell.[78] Both these attitudes are mistaken. Homeric characterisation not only exists, but is extraordinarily skilful, if its distinctive qualities, and with them the gulf that separates it from characterisation in the modern novel, are properly understood.

Like Semonides' female types, Homer's main heroes have many qualities in

[76] The principle is stated by Aristotle, *Poetics* 1449b36–1450a10 and 1454a16–b18; it is easily observable in the practice of Greek authors. The best English translation of the *Poetics* is that by M. E. Hubbard in D. A. Russell and M. Winterbottom, *Ancient Literary Criticism*, 1972.

[77] *Die dramatische Technik des Sophokles*, 1917; see H. Lloyd-Jones, *Classical Quarterly* 22, 1972, 214 for a description of this important book and its influence.

[78] See in particular *Die Entdeckung des Geistes*, 3rd edn., 1955 (translated by T. G. Rosenmeyer as *The Discovery of the Mind*, 1953). My book *The Justice of Zeus* (1971) attacks this theory.

Introduction

common; courage, determination and resourcefulness are obvious cases in point. Yet none is colourless and each is clearly distinct from every other. The differences between, say, Agamemnon, Nestor and Odysseus are comparatively clear. More remarkable is the differentiation between characters who, on the face of it, are very like each other; for example, that between Achilles, Ajax and Diomedes. By far the most elaborate characterisation in the *Iliad* is that of Achilles; even in our own time so hostile to individuality even in literature, the remarkably idiosyncratic character of his way of speaking has not failed to be observed. Another full characterisation is that of Hector. In the *Odyssey*, the personality of the hero himself is sketched in the richest detail; how distinctive are his curiosity and his vanity! He has to explore the island of the Cyclopes and the island of Circe, he must meet Polyphemus and see what kind of presents he makes to his guests, he must return to Circe's house; he is so vain that he must tell Polyphemus his true name, thus making it possible for his enemy to curse him. The whole subject of Homeric characterisation needs a new detailed study, which the late Adam Parry was already working at before his death in 1971.[79]

Drama had less space for extended characterisation than the epic; we should remember how much shorter the average Greek tragedy is than the average Elizabethan play. Yet the basic principles of characterisation are the same for the tragedians as they are for Homer. The character must be shown as being the sort of person to act as he acts in the story; action comes first and character comes later. Individual idiosyncrasy is not important; what are important are the basic emotions and the qualities that relate to them, such as pride, generosity, and honesty and their opposites. Eteocles and Agamemnon have complicated parts to play in the action; each is a noble hero, yet at the same time the inheritor of a family curse. Clytemnestra has a distinctive character, for her actions are exceptional. Orestes too performs an exceptional action; but he has no choice but to act as he does, and though his emotions are registered with the usual Aeschylean verisimilitude, he lacks distinctive colour.

[79]There are good remarks about character in Homer in Walter Marg's book (cited above, n. 57), 43 f. When Marg wrote (76), 'We only have to evoke in memory the figures of the epic heroes to recognise that the men of the epic are real individuals, who have a self, act quite on their own and have private mental processes', he was warned by a reviewer that this did not accord with the results attained by scholarship (see H. Diller, cited below, p. 104, n. 3.) These results consist in the theory advocated by scholarship (see the last note); they seem to me in no way to invalidate the justice of Marg's observations.

31

Females of the Species

In Sophocles the heroic characters are set against characters who are unheroic; Ajax contrasts with Odysseus, Antigone with Ismene, Electra with Chrysothemis, the first Oedipus with Creon. Some Sophoclean figures, particularly among the heroic characters, are delineated with great richness of detail; one thinks especially of the two Oedipuses, of Electra, and of Philoctetes. But in these plays, as in those of Aeschylus, the basic human emotions count for almost everything, psychological nicety for its own sake for nothing. This is not to condemn as irrelevant the rich psychological detail found, to take the examples chosen by John Bayley[80] for his brilliant defence of the autonomy of character in literature, in Chaucer, in Shakespeare or in Henry James; it is simply to point out that the characterising technique of the brief and austere tragedies of the Greeks was different.

Characterisation both in the Old and in the New Comedy is again governed by the basic principle that the character must be such as to act as the story tells us that he acted; but the nature of the genre entails certain differences. In the Old Comedy exaggeration, and not truth to nature, is an important feature. The characteristics of the ordinary Athenian are vastly magnified in the 'old man' who is the standard comic hero; extreme selfishness, cowardice, and sensuality combine with extreme self-confidence, resourcefulness and good fortune to make a Dicaeopolis or a Peisetaerus. Just so the lesser figures are types shaped to discharge their special function in the action. New Comedy is in this respect, as in several others, more akin to tragedy; the characters may be classifiable according to the obvious types, but they are subtly differentiated, each in accordance with the special requirements of the action of the play which he belongs to. The element of caricature survives in figures with a ruling passion, like the misanthrope, the flatterer, the superstitious man, who occur in a number of the plays; from such characters we may look aside to Theophrastus or back through the Old Comedy to Semonides.

In the light of this sketch the literary purpose of Semonides should be seen more clearly. It was not his purpose to supply an exhaustive catalogue of the chief types of feminine psychology. Rather he wished to entertain his audience by exploiting an observed resemblance between certain kinds of woman and certain kinds of animal, and by making use of this to argue the case in favour of the familiar thesis that the biggest plague to man is woman. The familiarity of this

[80] See John Bayley, *The Characters of Love*, 1960.

thesis to the Greeks, and its occurrence in the far more important and far more serious poetry of Hesiod, certainly tells us something about the Greek male attitude to women. But it would be unwise to take it as an exhaustive summary of the attitude towards them even of the men of Semonides' own society, time and place; and to get the best value from it we must combine it with other evidence, both from literature and from other sources. We have seen that in other Greek literature also one encounters the kind of character-study, or caricature, that makes play with the ruling passion, the dominant characteristic, the prevailing humour; and we have seen that the authors who exploit it, even the eminent philosopher Theophrastus, do so for ends that are not entirely serious.

The Poem in Translation

In the beginning the god made the female mind separately. One he made from a long-bristled sow. In her house everything lies in disorder, smeared with mud, and rolls about the floor; and she herself unwashed, in clothes unlaundered, sits by the dungheap and grows fat.

Another he made from a wicked vixen; a woman who knows everything. No bad thing and no better kind of thing is lost on her; for she often calls a good thing bad and a bad thing good. Her attitude is never the same.

Another he made from a bitch, vicious, own daughter of her mother, who wants to hear everything and know everything. She peers everywhere and strays everywhere, always yapping, even if she sees no human being. A man cannot stop her by threatening, nor by losing his temper and knocking out her teeth with a stone, nor with honeyed words, not even if she is sitting with friends, but ceaselessly she keeps up a barking you can do nothing with.

Another the Olympians moulded out of earth, a stunted creature; you see, a woman like her knows nothing, bad or good. The only work she understands is eating; and not even when the god makes cruel winter weather does she feel the cold and draw a stool near to the fire.

Another he made from the sea; she has two characters. One day she smiles and is happy; a stranger who sees her in the house will praise her, and say, 'There is no woman better than this among all mankind, nor more beautiful.' But on another day she is unbearable to look at or come near to; then she raves so that you can't approach her, like a bitch over her pups, and she shows herself ungentle and contrary to enemies and friends alike. Just so the sea often stands without a tremor, harmless, a great delight to sailors, in the summer season; but often it raves, tossed about by thundering waves. It is the sea that such a woman most resembles in her temper; like the ocean, she has a changeful nature.

Another he made from an ash-gray ass that has suffered many blows; when compelled and scolded she puts up with everything, much against her will, and does her work to satisfaction. But meanwhile she munches in the back room all night and all day, and she munches by the hearth; and likewise when she comes to the act of love, she accepts any partner.

Another he made from a ferret, a miserable, wretched creature; nothing about her is beautiful or desirable, pleasing or lovable. She is mad for the bed of love, but she makes any man she has with her sick. She does great damage to neighbours by her thieving, and often eats up sacrifices left unburned.

Another was the offspring of a proud mare with a long mane. She pushes servile work and trouble on to others; she would never set her hand to a mill, nor pick up a sieve nor throw the dung out of the house, nor sit over the oven dodging the soot; she makes her husband acquainted with Necessity. She washes the dirt off herself twice, sometimes three times, every day; she rubs herself with scents, and always has her thick hair combed and garlanded with flowers. A woman like her is a fine sight for others, but for the man she belongs to she proves a plague, unless he is some tyrant or king [who takes pride in such objects].

Another is from a monkey; this is the biggest plague of all that Zeus has given to men. Her face is hideous; when a woman like her goes through the town, everyone laughs at her. She is short in the neck; she moves awkwardly; she has no bottom, and is all legs. Hard luck on the poor man who holds such a misery in his arms! She knows every trick and twist, just like a monkey; she does not mind being laughed at, and will do no one a good turn, but considers, and spends the whole day planning, how she can do someone the worst possible harm.

Another is from a bee; the man who gets her is fortunate, for on her alone blame does not settle. She causes his property to grow and increase, and she grows old with a husband whom she loves and who loves her, the mother of a handsome and reputable family. She stands out among all women, and a godlike beauty plays about her. She takes no pleasure in sitting among women in places where they tell stories about love. Women like her are the best and most sensible whom Zeus bestows on men.

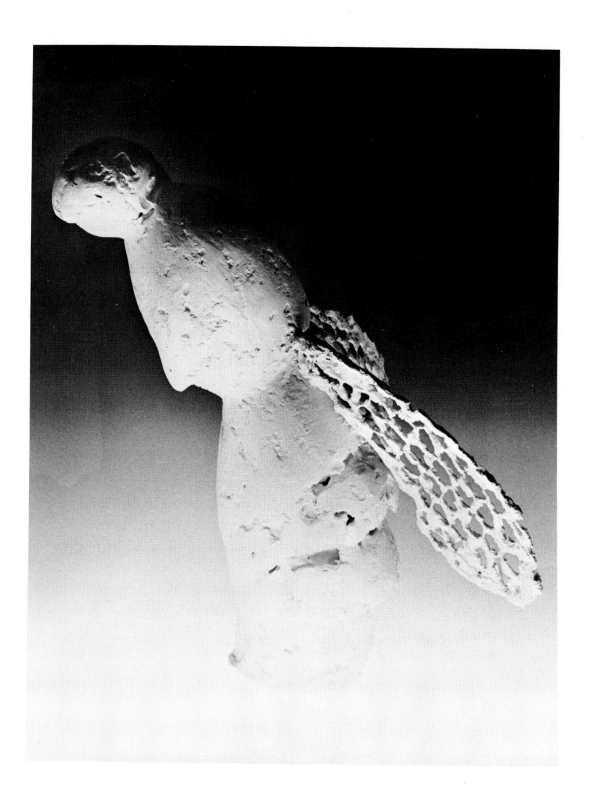

Zeus has contrived that all these tribes of women are with men and remain with them. Yes, this is the worst plague Zeus has made—women; if they seem to be some use to him who has them, it is to him especially that they prove a plague. The man who lives with a woman never goes through all his day in cheerfulness; he will not be quick to push out of his house Starvation, a housemate who is an enemy, a god who is against us. Just when a man most wishes to enjoy himself at home, through the dispensation of a god or the kindness of a man, she finds a way of finding fault with him and lifts her crest for battle. Yes, where there is a woman, men cannot even give hearty entertainment to a guest who has come to the house; and the very woman who seems most respectable is the one who turns out guilty of the worst atrocity; because while her husband is not looking . . . and the neighbours get pleasure in seeing how he too is mistaken. Each man will take care to praise his own wife and find fault with the other's; we do not realise that the fate of all of us is alike. Yes, this is the greatest plague that Zeus has made, and he has bound us to them with a fetter that cannot be broken. Because of this some have gone to Hades fighting for a woman. . . .

The Text

χωρὶς γυναικὸς θεὸς ἐποίησεν νόον
τὰ πρῶτα. τὴν μὲν ἐκ συὸς τανύτριχος,
τῆι πάντ᾽ ἀν᾽ οἶκον βορβόρωι πεφυρμένα
ἄκοσμα κεῖται καὶ κυλίνδεται χαμαί·
αὐτὴ δ᾽ ἄλουτος ἀπλύτοις ἐν εἵμασιν
ἐν κοπρίηισιν ἡμένη πιαίνεται.

    τὴν δ᾽ ἐξ ἀλιτρῆς θεὸς ἔθηκ᾽ ἀλώπεκος
γυναῖκα πάντων ἴδριν· οὐδέ μιν κακῶν
λέληθεν οὐδὲν οὐδὲ τῶν ἀμεινόνων·
τὸ μὲν γὰρ αὐτῶν εἶπε πολλάκις κακόν,
τὸ δ᾽ ἐσθλόν· ὀργὴν δ᾽ ἄλλοτ᾽ ἀλλοίην ἔχει.

    τὴν δ᾽ ἐκ κυνός, λιτοργόν, αὐτομήτορα,
ἢ πάντ᾽ ἀκοῦσαι, πάντα δ᾽ εἰδέναι θέλει,
πάντηι δὲ παπταίνουσα καὶ πλανωμένη
λέληκεν, ἢν καὶ μηδέν᾽ ἀνθρώπων ὁρᾶι.
παύσειε δ᾽ ἄν μιν οὔτ᾽ ἀπειλήσας ἀνήρ,
οὐδ᾽ εἰ χολωθεὶς ἐξαράξειεν λίθωι
ὀδόντας, οὐδ᾽ ἂν μειλίχως μυθεόμενος,
οὐδ᾽ εἰ παρὰ ξείνοισιν ἡμένη τύχηι,
ἀλλ᾽ ἐμπέδως ἄπρηκτον αὑονὴν ἔχει.

    τὴν δὲ πλάσαντες γηΐνην Ὀλύμπιοι
ἔδωκαν ἀνδρὶ πηρόν· οὔτε γὰρ κακὸν
οὔτ᾽ ἐσθλὸν οὐδὲν οἶδε τοιαύτη γυνή·
ἔργων δὲ μοῦνον ἐσθίειν ἐπίσταται.
κοὐδ᾽ ἢν κακὸν χειμῶνα ποιήσηι θεός,
ῥιγῶσα δίφρον ἆσσον ἕλκεται πυρός.

    τὴν δ᾽ ἐκ θαλάσσης, ἣ δύ᾽ ἐν φρεσὶν νοεῖ·

Codd. Stobaei SMA

1. γυναῖκας vel -ῶν Koeler: γυναῖκας . . . νόωι Ahrens γυναῖκας . . . νόου Meineke Ζεὺς Maas
2. ἐκ συὸς West: ἐξ ὑὸς codd. 4. κυλίνδεται cod. Paris. 1985: κυλινδεῖται SMA 5. αὕτη S
ἄλουτος Valckenaer: ἄπλυτος SMA ἀπλύτοισιν ἐν Wilamowitz ἱμάσιν fere codd. 6. ἡμένη
Trincavelli: εἱμένη fere codd. κακον (sine accentu) M 10. τὸν . . . αὐτὸν Schneidewin: τὸ . . .
αὐτὸν Wilhelm εἶ S κακῶν SM, A ante corr. 11. τὸν Schneidewin 12. λιτουργόν Gesner
λίταργον Wakefield αὐτομήτορα obscurum 16. ἄμμιν SM 18. οὔτ᾽ Bergk μυθεόμενος Fick:
μυθεύμενος codd. 19. ἡμένη Trincavelli: εἱμένη fere codd. 20. αὑονὴν S: αὖον ἢν M: αὖον ἢ
A: αὑονὴν West 24. ἔργον A 25. κοὐδ᾽ ἢν Schneidewin: χ᾽ οταν S: κοὔτ᾽ ἄν MA: κὤταν
Ahrens: χὤταν [sic] Trincavelli 26. ἆσσον Jacobsohn: ἄσσον codd. 27. δίχ᾽ noluit Schnei-
dewin

τὴν μὲν γελᾶι τε καὶ γέγηθεν ἡμέρην·
ἐπαινέσει μιν ξεῖνος ἐν δόμοις ἰδών·
30   "οὐκ ἔστιν ἄλλη τῆσδε λωΐων γυνὴ
ἐν πᾶσιν ἀνθρώποισιν οὐδὲ καλλίων"·
τὴν δ' οὐκ ἀνεκτὸς οὐδ' ἐν ὀφθαλμοῖς ἰδεῖν
οὔτ' ἄσσον ἐλθεῖν, ἀλλὰ μαίνεται τότε
ἄπλητον ὥσπερ ἀμφὶ τέκνοισιν κύων,
35   ἀμείλιχος δὲ πᾶσι κἀποθυμίη
ἐχθροῖσιν ἶσα καὶ φίλοισι γίνεται·
ὥσπερ θάλασσα πολλάκις μὲν ἀτρεμὴς
ἕστηκ', ἀπήμων, χάρμα ναύτηισιν μέγα,
θέρε̱ος ἐν ὥρηι, πολλάκις δὲ μαίνεται
40   βαρυκτύποισι κύμασιν φορε̱ομένη.
ταύτηι μάλιστ' ἔοικε τοιαύτη γυνὴ
ὀργήν· φυὴν δὲ πόντος ἀλλοίην ἔχει.
      τὴν δ' ἔκ τεφρῆς τε καὶ παλιντριβέ̱ος ὄνου,
ἣ σύν τ' ἀνάγκηι σύν τ' ἐνιπῆισιν μόγις
45   ἔστερξεν ὧν ἅπαντα κἀπονήσατο
ἀρεστά· τόφρα δ' ἐσθίει μὲν ἐν μυχῶι
προνὺξ προῆμαρ, ἐσθίει δ' ἐπ' ἐσχάρηι.
ὁμῶς δὲ καὶ πρὸς ἔργον ἀφροδίσιον
ἐλθόντ' ἑταῖρον ὁντινῶν ἐδέξατο.
50   τὴν δ' ἐκ γαλῆς, δύστηνον οἰζυρὸν γένος·
κείνηι γὰρ οὔ τι καλὸν οὐδ' ἐπίμερον
πρόσεστιν οὐδὲ τερπνὸν οὐδ' ἐράσμιον.
εὐνῆς δ' ἀληνής ἐστιν ἀφροδισίης,
τὸν δ' ἄνδρα τὸν παρε̱όντα ναυσίηι διδοῖ.
55   κλέπτουσα δ' ἔρδει πολλὰ γείτονας κακά,

29. μιν Valckenaer: μὲν codd.   30. λωΐων Gesner: λώϊον codd.   31. κάλλιον M   32. οὔτ' ἐν
Schneidewin   33. ἄσσον Jacobsohn: ἆσσον codd.   37–42. del. Jordan   37. ἀτρέμας
Valckenaer   40. φορεομένη Fick: φορευμένη codd.   42. δ' ὡς Grotius versum del.
Schneidewin   43. τεφρῆς τε Brunck (τε τεφρῆς Meineke): τε σποδιῆς codd.: alii alia   45.
ἔστερξεν A: ἔρερξεν M: ἔερξεν S   κἀπονήσατο Ahrens: καὶ πονήσατο codd.   49. ἐλθόνθ' S:
ἐλθόνδ' MA: ἐλθοῦσ'? ὁντινῶν Bergk: ὁντινοῦν codd.   50. γαλέης Welcker   51. οὔτε S ante
corr.   53. ἀληνής Bergk: ἀληνὴς S: ἀληνῆς codd. ceteri: ἀδηνής Winterton   54. παρε̱όντα
Renner: παρόντα codd.   διδοῖ Trincavelli: διδεῖ S: δίδει MA

ἄθυστα δ' ἱρὰ πολλάκις κατεσθίει.

    τὴν δ' ἵππος ἁβρὴ χαιτέεσσ' ἐγείνατο,
ἣ δούλι' ἔργα καὶ δύην περιτρέπει,
κοὔτ' ἂν μύλης ψαύσειεν, οὔτε κόσκινον
60   ἄρειεν, οὔτε κόπρον ἐξ οἴκου βάλοι,
οὔτε πρὸς ἰπνὸν ἀσβόλην ἀλεομένη
ἵζοιτ'. Ἀνάγκηι δ' ἄνδρα ποιεῖται φίλον·
λοῦται δὲ πάσης ἡμέρης ἄπο ῥύπον
δίς, ἄλλοτε τρίς, καὶ μύροις ἀλείφεται,
65   αἰεὶ δὲ χαίτην ἐκτενισμένην φορεῖ
βαθεῖαν, ἀνθέμοισιν ἐσκιασμένην.
κᾱλὸν μὲν ὦν θέημα τοιαύτη γυνὴ
ἄλλοισι, τῶι δ' ἔχοντι γίνεται κακόν,
ἢν μή τις ἢ τύραννος ἢ σκηπτοῦχος ἦι,
70   ὅστις τοιούτοις θυμὸν ἀγλαΐζεται.

    τὴν δ' ἐκ πιθήκου· τοῦτο δὴ διακριδὸν
Ζεὺς ἀνδράσιν μέγιστον ὤπασεν κακόν.
αἴσχιστα μὲν πρόσωπα· τοιαύτη γυνὴ
εἶσιν δι' ἄστεος πᾶσιν ἀνθρώποις γέλως·
75   ἐπ' αὐχένα βραχεῖα. κινεῖται μόγις,
ἄπυγος, αὐτόκωλος. ἆ τάλας ἀνὴρ
ὅστις κακὸν τοιοῦτον ἀγκαλίζεται.
δήνεα δὲ πάντα καὶ τρόπους ἐπίσταται
ὥσπερ πίθηκος· οὐδέ οἱ γέλως μέλει·
80   οὐδ' ἄν τιν' εὖ ἔρξειεν, ἀλλὰ τοῦτ' ὁρᾶι
καὶ τοῦτο πᾶσαν ἡμέρην βουλεύεται,
ὅκως τιν' ὡς μέγιστον ἔρξειεν κακόν.

    τὴν δ' ἐκ μελίσσης· τήν τις εὐτυχεῖ λαβών·
κείνηι γὰρ οἴηι μῶμος οὐ προσιζάνει,
85   θάλλει δ' ὑπ' αὐτῆς κἀπαέξεται βίος,
φίλη δὲ σὺν φιλέοντι γηράσκει πόσει
τεκοῦσα καλὸν κὠνομάκλυτον γένος.

---

56. cit. Athen. 179 D ἄθυτα Athen. ἱερά A, Athen. epit.   57–70. cit. Aelian., HA 16, 24   57. χαιτέεσσ' Meineke: χαιτάεσσ' Aelian: χαιτείης S: χαιτήεις MA   58. δύην: ἄτην Aelian. περιτρέχει Lattimore: παρατρέπει Koeler: alii alia   61. ἰπνὸν cod. Paris. 1985: ἴπνον MA: ἵππον S ἀλεομένη Fick: ἀλευμένη libri   65. αἰεὶ Hertel: ἀεὶ libri   67. ὦν Brunck: οὖν libri θέημα codd. Aelian.: θέαμα codd. Stob.   68. γίνεται A: γίγνεται SM   69–70. del. Page: an v. 70 tantum delendus est?   70. τοιοῦτον codd. Aelian.   73. αἴσχετα M   74. ἀστοῖσιν Ahrens: 75. ἀπ' αὐχένος Diels   76. αὐόκωλος Haupt ἦ τάλας Grotius: ἀταλας AS: ἀτάλης M   82. ὅκως S: ὅππως M: ὅπως A τιν' ὡς Meineke: τί χ' ὡς fere codd. (τι κῶς West)   86. συμ codd.: fort. σὺμ φιλέοντι: -εῦντι codd. πόσι Fick   87. κὠνομάκλυτον Smyth: κοὖν- codd.

58

κἀριπρεπὴς μὲν ἐν γυναιξὶ γίνεται
πάσῃσι, θείη δ' ἀμφιδέδρομεν χάρις.
90 οὐδ' ἐν γυναιξὶν ἥδεται καθημένη
ὅκου λέγουσιν ἀφροδισίους λόγους.
τοίας γυναῖκας ἀνδράσιν χαρίζεται
Ζεὺς τὰς ἀρίστας καὶ πολυφραδεστάτας.
    τὰ δ' ἄλλα φῦλα ταῦτα μηχανῆι Διὸς
95 ἔστίν τε πάντα καὶ παρ' ἀνδράσιν **μένει.**
Ζεὺς γὰρ μέγιστον τοῦτ' ἐποίησεν κακόν,
γυναῖκας· ἤν τι καὶ δοκέωσιν ὠφελεῖν
ἔχοντι, τῶι μάλιστα γίνεται κακόν·
οὐ γάρ κοτ' εὔφρων ἡμέρην διέρχεται
100 ἄπασαν, ὅστις σὺν γυναικὶ †πέλεται,
οὐδ' αἶψα Λιμὸν οἰκίης ἀπώσεται,
ἐχθρὸν συνοικητῆρα, δυσμενέα θεόν.
ἀνὴρ δ' ὅταν μάλιστα θυμηδεῖν δοκῆι
κατ' οἶκον, ἢ θεοῦ μοῖραν ἢ ἀνθρώπου χάριν,
105 εὑροῦσα μῶμον ἐς μάχην κορύσσεται.
ὅκου γυνὴ γάρ ἐστιν οὐδ' ἐς οἰκίην
ξεῖνον μολόντα προφρόνως δεκοίατο.
ἥτις δέ τοι μάλιστα σωφρονεῖν δοκεῖ,
αὕτη μέγιστα τυγχάνει λωβωμένη·
110 κεχηνότος γὰρ ἀνδρός — οἱ δὲ γείτονες
χαίρουσ' ὁρῶντες καὶ τόν, ὡς ἁμαρτάνει.
τὴν ἦν δ' ἕκαστος αἰνέσει μεμνημένος
γυναῖκα, τὴν δὲ τουτέρου μωμήσεται·
ἴσην δ' ἔχοντες μοῖραν οὐ γινώσκομεν.
115 Ζεὺς γὰρ μέγιστον τοῦτ' ἐποίησεν κακόν,
καὶ δεσμὸν ἀμφέθηκεν ἄρρηκτον πέδην,
ἐξ οὗ τε τοὺς μὲν Ἀΐδης ἐδέξατο
γυναικὸς εἵνεκ' ἀμφιδηριωμένους

·   ·   ·   ·   ·

88. γίγνεται S   90. κατημένη Schneidewin   91. οἴκου A   94–5. del. Jordan
94. ταῦτα: πάντα Ribbeck (et 95 πῆμα, quod coniecerat Heyne) μηχανὴ Hoffmann   95. μενεῖ
Bergk   97. τε Meineke δοκέωσιν Ahrens: δοκῶσιν codd.   98. τῶ vel τῶι codd.: ἔχοντί τοι
Koeler (post Winterton) γίνεται ΜΑ: γγ̄ S (— γίνονται?)   100. πέλεται: alii alia: fort. ναιετᾶι
102. θεόν Grotius: θεῶν codd.   106. οἴκου A οἰκίην Koeler: οἰκίαν codd.   107. μολόντ' ἄν
Meineke: μολῶντα codd.: μολόντα Trincavelli   δεκοίατο Schneidewin: δεχοίατο codd.
108. τῶι Hermann   110. post ἀνδρός lacunam indicavit Schaefer   116. πέδην Crusius: πέδη vel
πέδηι codd.: πέδης Koeler (ἀρρήκτου πέδης Meineke)   117. γε Gaisford

Commentary

Commentary

Unlike fr. 1, which has ὦ παῖ in its first line, and unlike several of Archilochus' poems, this poem contains no address to any person. This is no reason for assuming that the poem must have started with such an address; and the opening does not indicate that anything had preceded it.

1. 'The god made woman's mind separately.' The sentence would be easier if the poet had written γυναῖκας . . . νόον or γυναικῶν . . . νόον (Koeler) or γυναῖκας . . . νόωι (Ahrens). But Marg and others defend γυναικὸς . . . νόον as a kind of collective expression.

χωρίς standing first and used emphatically in the sense of 'separately' is attested; cf. Sophocles, *O.C.* 808 χωρὶς τό τ' εἰπεῖν πολλὰ καὶ τὸ καίρια and *Tr. fr. adesp.* 560 Nauck² χωρὶς τὰ Μυσῶν καὶ Φρυγῶν ὁρίσματα, and see Fraenkel on Aeschylus, *Ag.* 926. But what does it mean? Most people think it means 'separately from each other'. Since ten descriptions of women each made from different material follow, this makes perfectly good sense. As a programmatic statement at the start it seems rather flat; yet it may be argued that this is a mark of Semonides' archaic style.

Blomfield on Aeschylus, *Ag.* 681 seems to have been the first to take the words to mean, 'The god made woman's mind separately [from man's]'; Edmonds in his translation follows him. This has the advantage of being a more significant opening statement. In a number of creation myths, including that of Genesis and Hesiod's Pandora myth, woman is created after man; in a number, she is created out of different material; this usually signifies that she is inferior.

Most scholars reject this view because they feel that 'from man's' is difficult to supply from the context. But the poet is a man, and the audience he addresses at the symposium where poems were performed consisted of men. Would it really have been so difficult for such an audience to understand by 'separately' 'separately *from us*'? The poem would then start with a more significant statement; and the slight awkwardness of γυναικὸς would be removed. For if the poet is contrasting the female with the male mind, it is natural for him to use a singular; if he is insisting that the various women were made out of different material, a plural would be expected. The usual view that χωρὶς means 'separate from each other'

63

may be correct; but sense and language alike incline me to think that it more probably means 'separate from man's mind'.

The Homeric use of νόος and its cognates is described by K. von Fritz, *Classical Philology* 38, 1943, 79 f.; the results are summarised in the same journal, 40, 1945, 223–5. 'The term νόος,' he writes—(40, 223), '. . . is used mainly where recognition of an object leads to the realisation of a situation . . . since the same situation may have a different "meaning" to persons of different character and circumstances of life, the notion develops that different persons or nations have different νόος. As these different meanings of a situation evoke different reactions to it, and since these reactions are typical of certain persons, νόος sometimes implies the notion of a specific "attitude". Thus Odysseus (*Od.* 1, 3) πολλῶν ἀνθρώπων ἴδεν ἄστεα καὶ νόον ἔγνω. A situation which deeply affects the individual often suggests a plan, so that the word acquires a volitional in addition to its intellectual aspect.' In this instance, the volitional aspect is obviously important; the woman's 'attitude' is clearly at least as important a part of her 'way of thinking' as is her 'intelligence', so that νόος means much the same as our 'character'. In Homer, the Phaeacians have and the Cyclopes lack a god-fearing νόος, Ajax and Achilles have an arrogant νόος.

θεὸς here means not 'God' (this usage has too many modern overtones to be acceptable in rendering early Greek) nor 'a god', but 'the god in question'. This is Zeus; see 21, 93, 96, 115. The vowels are in synizesis, and there is no need to read Ζεὺς, as Maas, *R.–E.* III A, 1929, 185 tentatively suggested.

τὰ πρῶτα means 'originally', 'first of all'; cf. *Il.* 1, 6 ἐξ οὗ δὴ τὰ πρῶτα διαστήτην ἐρίσαντε, 6, 489 = *Od.* 8,553 ἐπὴν τὰ πρῶτα γένηται, *Od.* 8, 268 ὡς τὰ πρῶτ' ἐμίγησαν, Hes. *Th.* 108 εἴπατε δ' ὡς τὰ πρῶτα θεοὶ καὶ γαῖα γένοντο, 113, etc.

2. ἐκ συὸς: West rightly points out that εξυος in the early manuscripts might represent either ἐξ ὑὸς or ἐκ συὸς. Homer prefers σῦς and uses ὗς only when the metre requires it, but in Herodotus and in Attic ὗς is preferred. In Greek one would expect the initial sigma to be lost; whether it survived or was reintroduced is disputed (see Schwyzer, *GGI* 308). C. D. Buck, *Comparative Grammar of Greek and Latin*, p. 132, and A. Meillet and J. Vendryes, *Traité de grammaire comparée*, p. 49, both think the sigma was preserved through word-groups like τοὺς σύας. The only other occurrence of the word in an Ionian iambographer is at Hipponax 114 B, where the manuscripts of Eustathius have συός: this leads me to print the sigma.

Commentary

Domestic pig-keeping goes very far back in history. Pork was highly valued in antiquity, perhaps more than any other meat. The filthy habits of pigs are of course mentioned in Greek literature, e.g. by Heraclitus 54 B D.-K. = 36 M. But shameless people are commonly called dogs, not pigs, in Greek literature; nor is the pig a byword for greed so much as for mindless violence. This character must derive not from the domestic pig, but from the wild boar, which was hunted by the Greeks all through the classical period and later. The pig is not ἀναιδής, but ἀναίσθητος. The Greek for 'a bull in a china shop' is ὗς διὰ ῥόδων (see M. G. Bonanno, *Studi su Cratete Comico*, 1972, 67); the Alexandrian crowd at Theocritus 15, 72 shove 'like pigs' (see Gow ad loc.): Boeotians were called pigs, and the various forms of the proverb 'the pig once disputed with Athene' contrast stupidity with intelligence. F. H. Sandbach in Gomme and Sandbach, *Menander: A Commentary*, 458, is doubtless right in thinking that 'the wild boar on the mountain' is a type of unsocial ill-temper. See O. Keller, *Die antike Tierwelt*, 1909–13 (reprinted 1961), 388 f.

τανύθριξ means 'long-bristled'; Hesiod, *Op.* 516 applies it to a long-haired goat, Pseudo-Oppian, *Cyneg.* 1 187 to a horse's tail. Verdenius takes it to mean 'sharp-bristled', quoting τανύφυλλος, τανυήκης, τανυγλώχις. But in all these cases 'long' makes sense, and that is what one would expect a prefix derived from an extinct adjective but influenced in its meaning in compounds by τείνω (see Frisk, *EW* s.v., p. 852) to mean. Pigs in Greece and the Balkans have long bristles.

3. Marg and Verdenius both think the poet writes as if the animal and the woman were the same; Marg thinks this is a poetical contrivance, Verdenius calls it a survival of a naive habit of drawing no distinction in such cases. But, whether τῆι is relative or demonstrative, it may easily refer to τὴν.

βορβόρωι: this onomatopoeic word for mud is more pejorative than πηλός. It occurs first in the early iambographers: *Adesp. Iamb.* 9, 2 βορβ[ορ, Hipponax 135 B βορβορόπη(?), id. 29 A βορβορύζω. In the fifth century we find it in an elegiac fragment of Asius (14, 4) whose tone is markedly lower than that usual in elegiac verse, as well as in comedy. A Manichaean Gnostic sect called itself the βορβορῖται.

The basic sense of φύρω is to mix something dry with something wet; Homer uses it of tearstains (*Il.* 24, 162) and of bloodstains (*Od.* 9, 397). Hesiod, *Op.* 61 says Hephaestus was ordered to γαῖαν ὕδει φύρειν in order to create Pandora.

65

4. ἄκοσμος is found once in Homer, of Thersites (*Il.* 2, 213 ἄκοσμά τε πολλά τε ἤδη.

The three main manuscripts of Stobaeus give the form κυλινδεῖσθαι, commoner in prose. In Homer κυλίνδεσθαι always satisfied the metre, and therefore this form should be preferred; the early manuscripts will not have distinguished between them.

5. λούομαι means 'bathe', νίζω 'wash the hands or feet' and is used of washing clothes or linen. Sense as well as metre requires Valckenaer's correction. ἄλουτος recurs at fr. 10 A.

6. κοπρίῃσιν: in Homer Priam in his misery after Hector's death lies κυλινδό-μενος κατὰ κόπρον (*Il.* 22, 414; cf. 24, 163–4). I suppose the sow-woman sits near rather than on the dungheap; her purpose in doing so may be to guzzle food that has been thrown away, but perhaps she is simply indifferent to her surroundings.

7. 'Wicked': cf. *Il.* 8, 361; 23, 595; Solon 13, 27. ἀλιτήριος is the form in prose and comedy.

ἔθηκε here is a synonym of ἐποίησε. In the cosmogony in Alcman 5 fr. 2 col. II Page, Thetis owes her prominent position to the similarity of her name to parts of this verb; see M. L. West, *Class. Quart.* 12, 1963, 154 f.

8. Early Greek constantly referred to skill in terms of knowing things, i.e. tricks or arts; when Prometheus (Hesiod, *Theog.* 616) or Sisyphus (Alcaeus, fr. 38a, 5) is called πολύιδρις, it is their cunning, not their wide knowledge that is referred to; see R. B. Onians, *The Origins of European Thought*, 2nd edn., 1954, 15 f. The following clause repeats the same thing in different words. Edmonds' translation 'who takes note of it all' is wrong; λέληθεν is a perfect, and denotes a state, not an action. Verdenius thinks that ἀμεινόνων has only a rhetorical sense, being put in for the sake of 'polar expression'; but a clever person, good or bad, has what Genesis calls 'knowledge of good and evil'; the difference between the good and the bad clever person lies in the use made of this knowledge.

10. L. 10 has often been emended, but it confirms this interpretation; the vixen-woman has knowledge of good and evil, but pretends that good is evil and evil good, like Milton's Satan, who says, 'Evil, be thou my good.' Schneidewin's

emendation (accepted by Marg, p. 12, but given up by him later, p. 105), gives an inferior sense.

11. ὀργήν: Verdenius well compares Theognis 213–16, where the poet urges Cyrnus to acquire the ὀργή of a polyp which takes on the colour of the rock to which it clings; just so Tyrtaeus 11, 8 says that the Spartans have learned to know the ὀργή of war, whose variability he goes on to describe. The word ὀργή connotes emotion; that is how it comes to mean 'passion, wrath, anger'; but the emotions change, and it can refer to the temper of a single person as the successive emotions colour it. ὀργή occurs first in *Hymn. Cer.* 205, where Iambe is said to have given pleasure to the ὀργαί of Demeter, and Hesiod, *Op.* 304 where women are said to be like drones in their ὀργή. Its use in much the same sense as τρόπος is common in Pindar and not unknown in tragedy. With the present passage, cf. Hesiod, *Op.* 483 ἄλλοτε δ' ἀλλοῖος Ζηνὸς νόος. For νόος see on l. 1; in different ways both νόος and ὀργή have come to mean 'character'.

Changeability of character is often ascribed to the fox; at Aristophanes, *Wasps* 1241 the verb ἀλωπεκίζειν means 'to be on both sides at once', and at Pindar, *Pyth.* 2, 76 slanderers are said to resemble the ὀργά of foxes. In Aesop the fox is the type of cunning; in at least two fables Archilochus identified himself with this beast. Cf. Solon 11, 5 and Plato, *Rep.* 365c; see Keller 1, 88.

12. Dogs like the pariahs of modern India scavenged about Greek towns, and from the earliest times the animal was the type of shamelessness. Its name figures in Achilles' insults to Agamemnon (*Il.* 1, 225) and in Helen's self-reproaches (3, 180; 6, 344). Greek herdsmen's dogs were formidable brutes in ancient times, as they are today; Odysseus on arriving at Eumaeus' hut would have been attacked by the dogs if he had not had the sense to stay absolutely still (*Od.* 14, 29 f.). Their epithet in that place bears reference to their infuriating barking: ὑλακόμωροι. In mythology the figures of Cerberus and Scylla show the same awareness of the dog's most disagreeable features. Not that the Greeks failed to appreciate their good points; Homer tells the story of the faithful dog Argos (*Od.* 17, 291 f.), and Plato wishes his guardians to emulate their loyalty (*Rep.* 416A, etc.); see Keller 1, 128 f.

Hesychius glosses λιτουργόν by κακοῦργον: Didymus (p. 180 Schmidt) ap. Ammonius (300 Nickau p. 79) explains λιτουργεῖν by κακὰ λέγειν. λιτοργός is simply the Ionic form of this adjective; West quotes ἀλοργός from a fourth-century inscription from Samos (*GDI* 5702), and see H. W. Smyth, *The Ionic*

Females of the Species

Dialect, 1894, 154, and F. Bechtel, *Die gr. Dialekte* III, 1924, 108. Emendation is not necessary, but the element λιτ- is puzzling. Marg and Verdenius think that from meaning 'simple' λιτ- came to mean 'bad' (cf. *schlicht* and *schlecht*), but independent evidence is lacking.

αὐτομήτορα is difficult. Marg takes it to mean 'just like her mother', i.e. just like the real bitch; for the metaphor of maternity, cf. l. 57. Verdenius objects that the analogy of other compounds beginning αὐτο- does not support this. αὐτοπάτωρ, for instance, means 'one who is his own father', and αὐτάδελφος means 'own brother'. He prefers to follow Fränkel in taking it to mean 'altogether the mother', and to refer it to the bitch's habit of barking when anyone comes near her cubs (see l. 34). But when mothers are mentioned, even if they are bitches, aggressiveness is not the first characteristic that comes to mind, and this view makes the sense of the epithet remarkably obscure. I suggest that just as αὐτόχθων originally meant 'sprung from earth itself' (thus F. Sommer, *Zur Geschichte der Nominalkomposition*, Abh. der Bayer. Akad., heft 27, 1948, 83), so this word means ἀπ' αὐτῆς τῆς μητρός: the sense is not 'her mother's own self', but 'her mother's own child'.

13–14.   The anaphoric repetition of parts of πᾶς to secure emphasis is as old as Homer; cf., e.g., *Il.* 1, 287 f., and see D. Fehling, *Die Wiederholungsfiguren und ihr Gebrauch bei den Griechen vor Gorgias*, 1969, 200, 213. Marg observes that the frequent use of πᾶς in the descriptions of the women's habits is typical of the poet's forthright way of speaking; it occurs twenty-four times in the poem. But it is by no means alien to the epic style, as Marg suggests.

14.   Πάντηι . . . παπταίνουσα: cf. *Od.* 12, 233.

15.   λέληκεν: a perfect describes not an action but a state, and this verb well describes the sustained barking of Scylla (*Od.* 12, 85) or the sustained note of a bird pursuing (*Il.* 22, 141) or being pursued (Hes., *Op.* 207).

17.   Cf. *Od.* 18, 28–9 χαμαὶ δέ τε πάντας ὀδόντας|γναθμῶν ἐξελάσαιμι. . . .

18.   οὐδ' is alternative to οὔτ', but there is no need to normalise with Bergk; the οὐδὲ 'gives the effect of climax in the second limb' (Denniston, *GP* 193). Cf. *Il.* 6, 343 μύθοισι . . . μειλιχίοισι.

Commentary

19.   The woman might be sitting with friends in her own house or in theirs. τύχηι (SA) is better than M's τύχοι: the verb refers not to remote possibility, but to a likely eventuality; see W. W. Goodwin, *Syntax of the Greek Moods and Tenses*, 1897, 172–3.

20.   αὐονήν: West writes this with a rough breathing, drawing attention to καθανανεῖ at Archilochus 107. Probably one should write αὐαίνεται at Archilochus 89, 3; cf. Solon 4, 35 αὐαίνει. αὐονή comes from αὐαίνω which means 'I dry'; everywhere else it means 'dryness', but here it must mean 'barking' (cf. αὖω and αὖ, used to denote a dog's bark at Aristophanes, *Wasps* 903). M. Leumann, *Mus. Helv.* 14, 1957, 50 f. = *Kleine Schriften* 258 f. thinks that Semonides connected αὖος with αὖω because of the sound and αὖον with αὖσε because of the sense, and so used αὐονή as though it came from αὖω. Homer, *Il.* 13, 441 denotes a dry, rasping sound by αὖον ἄϋσεν; cf. 12, 160 αὖον ἀϋτεῦν and 13, 409 καρφαλέον δέ οἱ ἀσπὶς ... ἄϋσεν.

ἄπρηκτον here means 'with which nothing can be done'; cf. *Od.* 12, 223 ἄπρηκτον ἀνίην.

ἔχει means 'keeps up'; cf. *Il.* 16, 105 πήληξ ... καναχὴν ἔχε, 16, 794 and 18, 495 αὐλοὶ φόρμιγγές τε βοὴν ἔχον.

21 f.   Why is the series of seven animals and one insect interrupted by the insertion of women made from earth and sea? H. Fränkel thinks that Semonides here reflects the ideas of his fellow-Ionian Thales, who derived everything from water; earth, he thinks, in early cosmology stood for inactivity and water for activity (op. cit., 236 f.; see also the article 'A Thought Pattern in Heraclitus', *American Journal of Philology* 59, 1938, 309 f., which appears in German in *Wege und Formen frühgriechischen Denkens*, 2nd edn., 1960, 253 f.; see in particular p. 332 = p. 275 f.). I see no reason to suppose that Semonides was influenced by anyone apart from Hesiod, who at *Op.* 60 describes how Zeus ordered Hephaestus to mix earth with water in order to create Pandora. Wanting to describe an utterly inert woman, with whom no known animal could correspond, Semonides remembered Hesiod. That was suggested by J. T. Kakridis in the article quoted above, p. 20 (see Μελέτες καὶ ἄρθρα, p. 25 f.); but the point had been seen as early as Welcker (art. cit., 386, 392). One does not have to know about philosophy to make an earth-woman inert, nor to follow her with a sea-woman who is always changing.

21–2. Ὀλύμπιοι: see on θεός in l. 1; it comes to the same thing. πηρόν, 'crippled', is here for the first time found used metaphorically to indicate incapacity; cf. Plato, *Phaedrus* 275A, Aristotle, *EN* 1099b19. The earth-woman's ignorance of good things and bad connotes lack of skills quite as much as lack of knowledge; see on l. 8 above. The vixen-woman knows good things and bad, but deliberately makes out one to be the other; the earth-woman is simply ignorant.

24. A's ἔργον may be right, but it may result from assimilation to the case of μοῦνον. Having no skill of any kind, the earth-woman can only eat, the one thing every living creature has to do.

25. Accepting Ahrens' modification of S's χ'ὅταν to κῶταν, Verdenius explains his text by saying that when she ought to be getting up the fire the earth-woman simply pulls up her own stool. But in that case the woman's reluctance to get up the fire has to be read into the text, and for her to pull up her stool is only natural. We need a negative, and that both M and A give us, though in a slightly corrupt form; it is easily changed to Schneidewin's κοὐδ' ἦν, an almost certain correction. So we get excellent sense; even in icy weather the earth-woman is too inert to warm herself. κακὸν χειμῶνα: cf. Hesiod, *Op.* 496 κακοῦ χειμῶνος. θεός is Zeus, who sends the weather; see M. P. Nilsson, *Geschichte der gr. Religion* I², 392–3.

26. Cf. *Od.* 19, 506 ἀσσοτέρω πυρὸς ἕλκετο δίφρον Ὀδυσσεύς. ἄσσον: Jacobsohn, *Philologus* 67, 1908, 345 f. restored the correct Ionic accent, found in cod. Venetus A of Homer; see Chantraine, *Grammaire Homérique* I, 190.

In many passages of ancient literature the sea figures as the type of duplicity; A. Lesky, *Thalatta*, 1947, 27 f. lists some of them.

27. The substantival use of δύο exists; cf. *Il.* 10, 224 σύν τε δύ' ἐρχομένω, *Od.* 14, 74 ἔνθεν ἑλὼν δύ' ἔνεικε, Sophocles, *El.* 1088 δύο φέρειν ἐν ἑνὶ λόγωι. Yet the alteration to δίχ' (discountenanced by Schneidewin in 1836, as West notes, but accepted by Meineke and Wilamowitz) may be right; δίχα is regular in sentences like *Od.* 16, 73 δίχα θυμὸς ἐνὶ φρεσὶ μερμηρίζει: at Sappho, fr. 51 Lobel and Page write δίχα μοι τὰ νοήματα after Aristaenetus 1, 6, but Chrysippus has δύο.

28. Often the calm sea with the sun shining on it is said to laugh. Cf. *Hymn. Cer.* 14 γαῖά τε πᾶσ' ἐγέλασσε καὶ ἁλμυρὸν οἶδμα θαλάσσης; Theognis, 9 f. ἐγέλασσε δὲ γαῖα πελώρη,| γήθησεν δὲ βαθὺς πόντος ἁλὸς πολιῆς; *Hymn. Ap.* 118 μείδησε δὲ γαῖ' ὑπένερθεν; Aeschylus, *P.V.* 89 f. ἀνήριθμον γέλασμα (of the waves).

Commentary

29. ἐπαινέσει: note the asyndeton, which Hiller wanted to remove by writing κἀπαινέσει. Rather than speak of 'asyndeton with consecutive significance', as Verdenius does, I should call this a case where the connection of thought is obvious, and the writer passes rapidly to the next sentence; see Denniston, *GP* xliii.

μέν *solitarium* would surprise between the μέν in l.28 and the answering δέ in l.32; we should expect μιν, which after μὲν in the line before could easily have been corrupted.

30. λωΐων: this Homeric comparative is probable at Solon 20, 2, and is frequent in Theognis. In tragedy it is uncommon, and in Attic prose occurs only in formulae handed down from sacral language such as λῷον καὶ ἄμεινον: see Wilamowitz on Euripides, *Heracles* 196.

32. Schneidewin's οὔτ᾽ἐν is unnecessary; see Denniston, *GP* 510. ἀνεκτός with a negative is Homeric; cf. *Il.* 1, 573; 10, 118, etc. So is the pleonasm ἐν ὀφθαλμοῖσ᾽ ἰδεῖν: cf. *Od.* 10, 385; Callinus 1, 20, etc.

33–4. ἆσσον ἐλθεῖν: see on l. 26. The expression can be used of sexual contact as in Aeschylus, fr. 286 Mette ὁ δ᾽ Ἀντικλείας ἆσσον ἦλθε Σίσυφος: but there is no reason to suppose this here.

μαίνεται so soon after οὐκ ἀνεκτὸς recalls *Il.* 8, 355 ὁ δὲ μαίνεται οὐκέτ᾽ ἀνεκτῶς, *Od.* 9, 350 σὺ δὲ μαίνεαι οὐκέτ᾽ ἀνεκτῶς. ἄπλητον means 'unapproachably'; cf. *Hymn. Cer.* 83 ἄπλητον . . . χόλον, and Hesiod, *Theog.* 315 ἄπλητον κοτέουσα (see Richardson and West ad loc.). The tragic form is ἄπλατος (see G. Björck, *Das Alpha Impurum und die tragische Kunstsprache*, 1950, 344); for the distinction between that and ἄπλαστος, see West on *Theog.* 151.

For the fierceness of the bitch guarding her puppies, cf. *Od.* 20, 14 f. ὡς δὲ κύων ἀμαλῇσι περὶ σκυλάκεσσι βεβῶσα|ἄνδρ᾽ ἀγνοιήσασ᾽ ὑλάει μέμονέν τε μάχεσθαι.

35. ἀμείλιχος . . . κἀποθυμίη: cf. *Il.* 9, 158 ἀμείλιχος ἠδ᾽ ἀδάμαστος, *ib.* 572. κἀποθυμίη: cf. *Il.* 14, 261 ἀποθύμια ἔρδοι and Hesiod, *Op.* 710, and also *Il.* 1, 562 ἀπὸ θυμοῦ|μᾶλλον ἐμοὶ ἔσεαι, and 23, 595 ἐκ θυμοῦ πεσέειν (imitated at Callimachus, fr. 260, 40–1).

36. In Homer and the iambographers ἴσος (= ϜίσϜος) has a long initial vowel.

71

37–42. This is the only section in which the poet introduces a description of the material from which the woman is made (37–40) and follows it with 'That is what this woman is like'; this led H. Jordan, *Hermes* 14, 1879, 280 f. to delete the lines. It may well be felt that the resemblance to the sea is clear enough from the preceding description. But there is nothing in the lines that seems unlike our author; and in dealing with a writer of his date, it is not reasonable to demand either complete symmetry or conformity with modern taste in any other way.

37. πολλάκις: for the anaphora with this word, cf. Fehling, op. cit. 199–200.

ἀτρεμὴς: cf. *Il.* 13, 438 ἀτρέμας ἑσταότα: cf. *Od.* 19, 212. The adverb is found eight times in Homer (ἀτρέμα once); the adjective occurs first here, and Valckenaer wanted to emend it; but Parmenides 1, 29 has ἀτρεμὲς ἦτορ. ἀτρεμέως occurs at Theognis 978.

38. ἕστηκ': cf. Virgil, *Ecl.* 2, 26 cum placidum ventis staret mare; Aeschylus, *Ag.* 565–6 πόντος ἐν μεσημβριναῖς|κοίταις ἀκύμων νηνέμοις εὕδει πεσών. ἀπήμων is used of the sea at Hesiod, *Op.* 670.

χάρμα stands here in apposition to the subject, as at *Il.* 10, 193 μὴ χάρμα γενώμεθα δυσμενέεσσιν, and is not an internal accusative attached to the verb, as at *Il.* 3, 51, where Paris is said to have brought Helen to Troy δυσμενέσιν . . . χάρμα.

39. θέρεος ἐν ὥρηι: cf. Hesiod, *Op.* 664 ἐς τέλος ἐλθόντος θέρεος, καματώδεος ὥρης.

μαίνεται is taken up from l. 33; the verb is used metaphorically of things in Homer, e.g., of fire at *Il.* 15, 606.

40. βαρυκτύποισι: this word is an epithet of Zeus at fr. 1, 1, and also twice in Hesiod and four times in *Hymn. Cer.*; it is used of Poseidon at Hesiod, *Theog.* 818 and Pindar, *Ol.* 1, 72 and *Paean* 4, 41.

φορεῖσθαι, like φέρεσθαι, may be used of rapid forward motion, and that is how Radermacher and Fränkel take the participle here; but it is better to follow Von Sybel in taking it as passive and not middle; the waves are said to 'fling the sea about', as at Euripides, *Hecuba* 29 the corpse of Polydorus is πολλοῖς διαύλοις κυμάτων φορούμενος.

42. ὀργήν: see on l. 11. Radermacher finds that the words in the manuscripts— φυὴν δὲ πόντος ἀλλοίην ἔχει—show a delightful old-fashioned naiveté; Marg finds them innocently comic; and others find them flat. On the face of it they mean, 'But the sea has a different sort of character.' Perhaps the poet is reminding us that

Commentary

the sea-women cannot resemble the sea quite as the women made from animals resemble these animals; but this may well seem feeble. Grotius inserted ὡς to get the sense, 'And like the sea she has a different sort of character.' That again is feeble; it would make sense if ἀλλοίην could mean 'changeable', but for that meaning ἄλλοτ' ἀλλοῖον, as in l. 11, would be required. Fränkel thought the word πόντος was corrupt.

This is a difficult problem; but I believe we can get adequate sense without emendation. At Herodotus 5, 40, 1 the Spartan ephors and elders warn Anaxandridas not to resist, ἵνα μή τι ἀλλοῖον περὶ σεῦ Σπαρτιῆται βουλεύσωνται. ἀλλοῖον is a euphemism, or meiosis, says R. W. Macan ad loc.; 'a decision of *another* character' will mean an unwelcome decision (thus also L.S.J. s.v. and J. E. Powell in his Herodotean lexicon). The use is rare; the only other instance quoted by L.S.J. is εἴ τι γένοιτο ἀλλοῖον, in a fragment of the third-century philosopher Arcesilaus quoted by Diogenes Laertius 4, 44. But the words ἕτερος and ἄλλος can be used with the same sinister implication underlying their basic sense of 'other'. Pindar, *Pyth.* 3, 34 says of Coronis δαίμων δ' ἕτερος ἐς κακὸν τρέψαις ἐδαμάσσατο νιν: Schroeder ad loc. rightly observes that ἕτερος is euphemistic. Just so at Aeschylus, *Ag.* 151 Calchas prays that Artemis may not hurry on θυσίαν ἑτέραν, ἄνομόν τιν', ἄδαιτον: and at *Suppl.* 635 f. I would retain μάχλον Ἄρη, τὸν ἀρότοις θερίζοντα βροτοὺς ἐν ἄλλοις and render 'in a different kind of ploughing'.

If ἀλλοίην here can bear this sinister sense, the meaning will be, 'And the sea has a nature unlike that of other things', i.e., a nature that is sinister and uncanny.

φυή, the Homeric word, recurs at Archilochus 25, 1; φύσις is not found in the iambographers, and in Homer only at *Od.* 10, 303.

43–9. The most famous mention of the ass in Greek literature is that in which Ajax, slowly retreating in the face of heavy Trojan pressure, is compared to an ass who has found his way into a cornfield and retires, still munching, as boys pound him with their cudgels (*Il.* 11, 558 f.):

> ὡς δ' ὅτ' ὄνος παρ' ἄρουραν ἰὼν ἐβιήσατο παῖδας
> νωθής, ὧι δὴ πολλὰ περὶ ῥόπαλ' ἀμφὶς ἐάγη
> κείρει τ' εἰσελθὼν βαθὺ λήϊον. οἱ δέ τε παῖδες
> τύπτουσιν ῥοπάλοισι. βίη δέ τε νηπίη αὐτῶν.
> σπουδῆι τ' ἐξήλασσαν, ἐπεί τ' ἐκορέσσατο φορβῆς.

'Beaten again and again' harmonises with this passage; the sense of 'crafty' which this word bears at Sophocles, *Phil.* 448 must derive from the notion of having been rubbed again and again (cf. Sophocles, *Ant.* 177 ἐντριβής, and the words τρίμμα and περίτριμμα).

The first epithet of the ass in l. 44 is corrupt. The word σπόδιος, bearing the appropriate sense of 'ash-gray' is attested, but the dactyl here is impossible. Presumably a gloss has ousted the correct word. The adjective τεφρός occurs at Herodas 7, 71 and Babrius 65, 1; Hesychius glosses it with σπόδ‹ι›ον, φαιόν, πολιόν, and the scholia on Nicander, *Ther.* 173 say τεφρῶδες καὶ σποδῶδες. This use by an imitator of the early iambus like Herodas recommends τεφρῆς: but other words for 'gray' cannot be ruled out. Brunck conjectured τεφρῆς τε, which Meineke modified to τε τεφρῆς. Meineke's slight gain in palaeographical neatness is offset by his less likely word order; for two adjectives of similar length linked by τε . . . καί, cf. Archilochus, fr. 176, 2 τρηχύς τε καὶ παλίγκοτος.

44. ἀνάγκηι here, as often, means 'compulsion' rather than 'necessity'. ἐνιπῆσιν: ἐνίπτω is a Homeric word which is found in drama only at Aeschylus, *Ag.* 590. 'Enipo' is a suspiciously apt name for Archilochus' mother (see Archilochus, fr. 295).

45. ἔστερξεν (gnomic aorist), 'has to put up with', gives just the right sense. On ὦν Verdenius quotes Denniston, *GP* 421, who speaks of instances in which οὖν is used 'to stress the correspondence between idea and fact, the objective reality of something which in the main clause is merely supposed'. But Denniston is speaking of the use with relatives, as his reference to 'the main clause' shows. More relevant here is the specifically Ionic use with compound verbs in tmesis, generally in the aorist and often in the gnomic aorist; Herodotus and the Hippocratic Corpus have many instances, but see also Callimachus, *Hy.* 6, 75; fr. 64, 5; fr. 384, 5. Cf. Denniston, *GP* 429 and Kühner-Gerth 1 p. 537. Denniston thinks this use may derive from Homeric οὖν referring to something foreshadowed, but notes that the earliest instances are not apodotic; he quotes Epicharmus, fr. 124 and fr. 35, 6 Kaibel, and we may now add Hipponax 78, 16. K.-G. suggest that the use derives from popular speech, and point out that it serves to present an action as energetic and lively or as sudden and immediate; this seems likelier than that it derives from Homer.

κἀπονήσατο: crasis seems likelier than Homeric omission of the augment. Homer has only the middle of this verb; so has Archilochus 42, 2 and 98, 15, the only other instances in the iambographers.

Commentary

46. τόφρα without a corresponding ὄφρα or ἕως occurs at *Il.* 10, 498; 13, 83; *Od.* 3, 303 and 464, etc.; and 'meanwhile' suits the sense.

ἐσθίει μὲν . . . ἐσθίει δέ: for similar anaphora, see Fehling, op. cit. 193. Are donkeys so greedy? Plato seems to have thought so (see *Phaedo* 81E), but I have heard it denied by people who know them well. Perhaps their continuous slow munching and their readiness to eat even thistles has given them this reputation; Semonides may have been influenced by the comparison of Ajax to an ass quoted above.

'μυχός has two senses, the particular sense of recess or corner and the general meaning of the inner rooms of the house': A. J. B. Wace, *Journal of Hellenic Studies* 71, 1951, 218. See the convenient plan reproduced on p. 203 of Wace's article; in front was the outer court, containing the altar of Zeus Herkeios; then came the megaron with the hearth (ἐσχάρη) at the back of it, then the women's quarters and at the back the μυχός. At *Od.* 4, 305 Arete sits spinning by the hearth, but at *Il.* 22, 440 the women are weaving in the μυχός.

47. προνὺξ προῆμαρ: J. Wackernagel, *Sprachliche Untersuchungen zu Homer*, 1916, 45, n. 1 says that the compound προῆμαρ results from the possibility of saying πρὸ ἦμαρ in the sense 'on and on each day'; he compares πρόπαν, used by Homer, apart from a single instance in the Catalogue of Ships (*Il.* 2, 498), only in the phrase πρόπαν ἦμαρ, in which προ could go with the entire sentence. M. Leumann, *Homerische Wörter*, 1950, 99 f. remarks that Semonides must have taken προπανῆμαρ as a single expression; he thinks the addition of προνὺξ was suggested by the phrase νύκτας τε καὶ ἦμαρ.

48–9. ὁμῶς: if ὁμῶς went with ὁντινῶν in the sense of 'any partner alike', we should expect it to come at the end of the sentence. If it means 'in the same way', the woman's insatiability where food is concerned is said to be matched by her insatiability, manifested in an utter lack of selectivity, in matters of love. It is not entirely easy to understand this, and Verdenius objects that the donkey-woman's constant eating, unlike her acceptance of any partner in love, is not a mark of indifference. But eating all the time comes very near to being ready to eat any-thing; the common factor in the woman's eating habits and sexual habits is that of insatiability. She is πάμφαγος in both senses.

The syntax would be a little easier if one read ἐλθοῦσ' in place of the manu-scripts' ἐλθόντ': the word could easily have been assimilated to the case of the

75

next word, ἑταῖρον. The sense would then be 'when she comes to the act of love', but perhaps the point is that 'the first comer' will do. For ἔργον ἀφροδίσιον, see *Hymn. Ven.* 1, 9 and the Hippocratic Oath (W. H. S. Jones, *Hippocrates* 1, Loeb Library, p. 300, l. 27); for ἑταῖρος in a sexual sense, cf. Aristophanes, *Eccl.* 992. The word order makes against its being predicative.

The ass seems to have owed the great reputation for lubricity which it enjoyed in ancient times to the large penis of the male. See Archilochus, fr. 43, 2; Priapus was represented as having an ass's genitals, and in his cult, originating at Lampsacus, but spreading to other parts of the Greek world, an ass was sacrified to him; see H. Herter, *De Priapo*, Religionsgeschichtliche Versuche und Vorarbeiten xxiii, 1932. But even Apollo had asses sacrificed to him, and delighted in their ithyphallic gambolling (Pindar, *Pyth.* 10, 32 f.; Callimachus, fr. 186, 10 with Pfeiffer's note).

On the ass in antiquity, see Keller 1, 259 f.

50.–6 Keller 1, 160 f. maintains that the weasel was the ordinary domestic mouse-killer of the ancient world as late as the fifth century B.C. If true, that is surprising. Since the reign of Psammetichus in the middle of the seventh century the Greeks had been in close contact with Egypt (see M. M. Austin, 'Greece and Egypt in the Archaic Age', *Proc. Camb. Phil. Soc.*, suppl. 2, 1970), and must have been familiar with the cat; and what civilised human being could prefer the weasel, with its foul smell and thievish habits, when a cat was available? Sylvia Benton, *Class. Rev.* 19, 1969, 260 has made a strong case (*contra* Gow on Theocritus 15, 28 and in *Class. Rev.* 17, 1967, 195) for thinking that in fifth-century Athens cats were not uncommon. Gisela Richter, *Animals in Greek Sculpture* 33, (with pl. lvi) notes five cats, but no weasels, in fifth- and fourth-century art; on an Attic pyxis (*ARV* 917) Furtwängler and Beazley concurred in finding two cats. Against this Aristophanes mentions weasels fourteen times and cats only once; but as Miss Benton remarks (p. 262) that need only mean that weasels seemed more comic; they figured in a number of common phrases, as the sections of J. Taillardat's book *Les Images d'Aristophane* listed s.v. γαλῆ will show.

The weasel was proverbial for darting about, for lasciviousness, for stealing and for stinking; see Keller 1, 164 f. and Marg in an article that will appear in *Hermes* 102, 1974, 151 f. But one feature of Semonides' γαλῆ hardly suits the domestic weasel: its extreme ugliness. The domestic weasel is rather a pretty little creature; but the ferret, called by the Greeks Ταρτησσία γαλῆ or ἀγρία γαλῆ, originating in Spain and

Commentary

North Africa and known to them as early as Herodotus (4, 192; cf. Strabo 144), is a repulsive-looking beast. A scholion on Nicander, *Ther.* 196 identifies the ἴκτις usually translated 'marten' with the ἀγρία γαλῆ and suggests that the creature of whose skin Dolon's cap was made (*Il.* 10, 335) was one of them; but that is most uncertain. Anyhow, the hideousness of Semonides' beast sounds more like the 'wild' or 'Tartessian' weasel, i.e. the ferret, than the ordinary variety.

50.   δύστηνος is a general word for 'miserable'; its occurrence leads Verdenius to observe that the beast's appearance was in general thought a bad omen (see E. K. Borthwick, *Class. Quart.* 18, 1968, 200 f.). It is a poetic word, common in epic and tragedy, in comedy found only in paratragoedic passages and occurring twice in Semonides (fr. 1, 12 and 18) and once in Archilochus (193). In all three instances in the iambographers the style is elevated; in 'Homerus' 7, 14 West the context is defective.

οἰζυρός is found in Homer meaning 'lamentable', but later acquires a semi-colloquial use. The tragedians and early Attic prose writers do not use it, but Aristophanes often has it in exclamations of pity, indignation or impatience (see Dover on *Clouds* 655). When Hesiod, *Op.* 639 applied the word to his native village, it may already have acquired this kind of connotation: cf. Archilochus 102 ὡς Πανελλήνων ὀϊζὺς ἐς Θάσον συνέδραμεν.

γένος might mean 'race', but is commonly enough applied to persons as γέννημα may be, in the sense of 'creature'; the epic use in phrases like θεῖον or δῖον γένος (*Il.* 6, 180, of the Chimaera; at *Il.* 9, 538, of Artemis; Hesiod, *Op.* 299, of Perses) or γένος βασιλήιον (*Od.* 16, 401, of Telemachus) is taken up by Sophocles, *Ajax* 784 ὦ δαΐα Τέκμησσα, δύσμορον γένος.

51.   We cannot help comparing Archilochus 22, 1 οὐ γάρ τι καλὸς χῶρος οὐδ' ἐπίμερος, but we must resist the temptation to speak of either passage as an 'echo' of the other. At Hesiod, *Theog.* 132 and *Aspis* 15 φιλότης is ἐφίμερος. ἵμερος, 'desirability', is conceived as a quality darted from the eyes of attractive persons.

52.   ἐράσμιος 'seems to be at home only in Ionic, and though it in no way has an indecent sense, in the sphere of the erotic in particular': Fraenkel on Aeschylus, *Ag.* 605, the only place where the word is found in Attic before Plato. In Anacreon 375, 1 Page it is an epithet of ἥβη.

53.   ἀληνής: this word is found nowhere else in a text, although Hesychius has the gloss ἀληνής· μαινόμενος and also ἀλινοί· ἐπαφρόδιτοι. The word may be

corrupt, and the gloss may derive from an already corrupt form; its etymology is not clear. But the sense 'mad', or at any rate 'mad for', seems preferable to that of ἀδηνής, which would mean 'unskilful', and ἀπηνής would not be easily construed with a genitive. *Contra* West, *SGEI*, 178.

54. τὸν ἄνδρα τὸν παρεόντα could mean 'whatever husband she has for the time being' or 'whatever man is with her'; since this makes good sense, we need not consider emendations.

ναυσίηι διδοῖ: cf. *Il.* 5, 397 ὀδύνηισιν ἔδωκεν: *Od.* 19, 167 ἀχέεσσί γε δώσεις: Pindar, *Pyth.* 5, 60 ἔδωκ' Ἀπόλλων θῆρας αἰνῶι φόβωι: Theocritus 7, 124 with Gow's note. ναυσίη is Ionic for Attic ναυτία. The weasel stinks; cf. Aristophanes, *Ach.* 255, *Plut.* 693.

55. κλέπτουσα: the weasel steals; cf. Aristophanes, *Thesm.* 559, *Pax* 1151, *Vesp.* 363.

56. The ferret-woman is a *bustirapa;* i.e. she helps herself to sacrificial offerings, near tombs or in other places, which have escaped burning; cf. Catullus 59, 2–3 (see Kroll ad loc.) and Terence, *Eun.* 491 (probably from Menander).

57 f. The immense importance of the horse in Greek culture and the high value attached to fine horses scarcely needs illustration; it is sufficient to refer to Keller 1, 218 f. and to J. K. Anderson, *Ancient Greek Horsemanship*, 1961. One famous passage of Homer, in particular, is relevant to the presentation of the mare-woman; at the end of the sixth book of the *Iliad*, Paris, going out to battle, is compared to a proud stallion (l. 506 f.):

> ὡς δ' ὅτε τις στατὸς ἵππος, ἀκοστήσας ἐπὶ φάτνηι,
> δεσμὸν ἀπορρήξας θείηι πεδίοιο κροαίνων,
> εἰωθὼς λούεσθαι ἐϋρρεῖος ποταμοῖο
> κυδιόων. ὑψοῦ δὲ κάρη ἔχει, ἀμφὶ δὲ χαῖται
> ὤμοις ἀΐσσονται. ὁ δ' ἀγλαΐηφι πεποιθώς,
> ῥίμφα ἑ γοῦνα φέρει μετά τ' ἤθεα καὶ νομὸν ἵππων.

Keeping horses was proverbially expensive; only the richest families of Greece could enter for the chariot and horse races at the Panhellenic games, in competition with monarchs like Hieron of Syracuse or Arcesilas of Cyrene. The troubles of

Commentary

Strepsiades, the chief character of Aristophanes' *Clouds*, are caused by his marriage with a perfect specimen of the mare-woman; see ll. 46–74.

ἀβρή means 'proud, luxurious, delicate'. The word is not found in Homer or in Hesiod, but is significantly frequent in early lyric. Sappho 58,25 says ἔγω δὲ φίλημμ' ἀβροσύναν: she applied the adjective to the Graces (128) and to Adonis (140, 1); she tells the cupbearer to pour the wine ἄβρως (2, 14), and Anacreon plays a musical instrument in this fashion (373, 2). In Alcaeus 42 it is an epithet of Thetis; in Anacreon it refers to the neck of the beautiful boy Smerdies (347, 1). Sometimes the word refers to a person's manner of walking; in Anacreon 461 ἀβρός is said to mean ὁ κούφως βαίνων, and ἀβροβάτης is applied to the delicately-stepping Oriental servant at Bacchylides 3, 48. Xenophanes 3,1 West says that the men of Colophon learned 'useless luxuriousnesses', ἀβροσύνας ἀνωφελέας, from the Lydians; Lydia was the chief source of luxury for Sappho's circle (see Page, *Sappho and Alcaeus*, 102–3). Cf. Verdenius, *Mnemosyne* 15, 1962, 392.

χαιτέεσσ': metre requires the form with the second vowel shortened before the long vowel that follows it. The word recurs in early poetry only in Phocylides, fr. 2, 3 (see below, Appendix II) and in Pindar, *Pyth.* 9, 5; for the shortening, cf. Archilochus 122, 8 ἠχέεντα. The mane has always been thought an important feature of equine beauty; cf. *Il.* 6, 509–10 (quoted in the last note).

περιτρέπειν is used of diverting blame or responsibility onto others; cf. Lysias 6,14 μὴ βούλεσθε εἰς ὑμᾶς τὴν αἰτίαν περιτρέψαι: Aristides 2,400D γυναῖκάς φασι τοῖς ἀνδράσι περιτρέπειν τὰ σφέτερ' αὐτῶν ἁμαρτήματα. I fail to see why the verb cannot, by a very natural extension, be used of 'pushing work onto' others; Fränkel's translation suggests that he takes it in this way. Koeler's παρατρέπει would mean 'turn aside' or 'divert'; Lattimore's περιτρέχει (*American Journal of Philology* 65, 1944, 172) would mean 'run round' or 'circumvent' (cf. Aristophanes, *Eq.* 56); Schneidewin's περιτρέμει, 'is afraid of', is less good. But no change is necessary.

59.   The handmill was used for pressing oil, but the commonest use of it was for grinding corn; see L. A. Moritz, *Grain-Mills and Flour in Classical Antiquity*, 1958, *passim*. For Homeric allusions to women grinding corn, see *Od.* 7, 104 and 20, 105 f.

Sieving was another part of the process; the *Geoponica* 2, 19, 5 mention a sieve made out of a wolf's hide with thirty holes, through each of which you could stick a finger; cf. *ib.* 15, 2, 12. The passage is well illustrated by the account of grinding (19 f.) and sieving (39 f.) given in the pseudo-Virgilian *Moretum*.

60. κόπρον: cf. l. 6; one used a dung-fork for this purpose.

The stove tended to be near the κοπρών (privy) (see D. S. Robertson, *Proc. Camb. Phil. Soc.*, 1938, 10, though his suggestion regarding Aristotle, *De Part. Anim.* 645a15–23 has been refuted by L. Robert, *Opera Minora Selecta*, 1968, iii, 1538 f.). But her distaste for soot is enough to explain the mare-woman's averseness to sitting over the stove, which an ordinary woman would presumably do in the course of cooking. Not surprisingly, ἰπνός does not occur in poetry except here and in comedy.

61. ἀλέομαι is a Homeric verb, not found later except in Hesiod and Theognis; at Aeschylus, *P.V.* 568 Wilamowitz' ἀλεῦμαι is not necessary.

62. Ἀνάγκηι . . . φίλον. Some have taken this to mean that she makes her husband love her only through the compulsion of sexual desire; but if that were so the nature of the compulsion would surely be more clearly indicated. Verdenius thinks it means that she takes a husband only because she has to; but this hardly suits the mare-woman, and ἄνδρα ποιεῖται φίλον would not express it very clearly. I much prefer Lattimore's view (art. cit. in n. on ll. 57 f., p. 173) that it means 'she makes her husband intimate with hard times'. On the allegorical personification of such figures as Penia, Amechania, Ananke, see H.-J. Newiger, *Metapher und Allegorie: Studien zu Aristophanes*, 163; Penia occurs at Hesiod, *Op.* 717 f.; Alcaeus 364 Page couples her with her sister Amechania. For Semonides this seems just right; cf. the personification of Famine in ll. 101–2; for instances of Ananke personified, see H. Schreckenberg, *Ananke*, 1964, 73 f., etc.

63. Washing in warm water was thought a luxury, especially in warm weather, even in fifth-century Athens; see Dover on Aristophanes, *Nub.* 837 and cf. 991 and 1044. The woman obviously washes in a private bath (cf. Aristophanes, *Pax* 842 f.); for these, see R. Ginouvès, *Balaneutike*, 1962, 151 f.

64. Perfumes were naturally expensive. They are mentioned in Homer only at *Il.* 14, 171 f. and *Od.* 18, 192 f. μύρον occurs first in Archilochus 48, 5 and 205, if not here or at Semonides 16, 1; see Page, *Sappho and Alcaeus*, 78–9. At Alcaeus 50, 1 and 362 and at Anacreon, fr. 363, men use it.

65. Cf. Archilochus 31 ἥ δέ οἱ κόμη|ὤμους κατεσκίαζε καὶ μετάφρενα and note βαθυχαίτης at Hesiod, *Theog.* 977.

Commentary

66. σκιάζω and its cognates are often used of people wearing garlands; cf. Aeschylus, *Ag.* 493–4. The mare-woman is garlanded, as though for a festival or a sacrifice, even on ordinary occasions; cf. L. Deubner, 'Die Bedeutung des Kranzes im klassischen Altertum', *Archiv für die Religionswissenschaft* 30, 1933. ἄνθεμον for ἄνθος occurs first at *Hymn. Hom.* 6, 9; Sappho 132, 1. Pindar has it at *Ol.* 2, 72 and *N.* 7, 79 and Aristophanes at *Ach.* 992 (in lyric); it does not occur in tragedy. Homer has ἀνθεμόεις, and M. Leumann, *Homerische Wörter* 49 thinks that ἄνθεμον was formed from this adjective on the analogy of ἠνεμόεις/ἄνεμος.

67. The ὦν is inferential, the μέν answered by δέ in the next line. ἔχειν is often used of a husband's having a woman as his wife; cf. e.g. *Od.* 4, 569. Aristippus said ἔχω Λαΐδα ἀλλ᾽ οὐκ ἔχομαι, according to Diogenes Laertius 2, 75. The chiastic order is effective.

69. Hippias (6 *FGH* fr. 6), cited in the hypothesis to Sophocles, *O.T.*, says that the word τύραννος came in in the time of Archilochus; τυραννίς occurs at fr. 19, 3 and τ[υραν]νίην seems probable at fr. 23, 20 of that author. This is probably the earliest instance of τύραννος: the Homeric Hymn to Ares (see *Hymn. Hom.* 8, 5) is attributed by M. L. West, *Class. Quart.* 20, 1970, 300 f. to Proclus in the fifth century A.D., and can hardly be much earlier. Alcaeus has three instances. The word is certainly of Oriental origin, but its etymology has been much disputed; see A. Heubeck, *Praegraeca* 68.

σκηπτοῦχος is Homeric, both in the phrase σ. βασιλεύς (*Il.* 1, 279; 2, 86, etc.) and alone (*Il.* 14, 93). Here it obviously means a king, as in Homer, and not, as L.S.J. seems to imply, an officer at the Persian court, first mentioned in Xenophon. 'Tyrant or king' is a distinction we may perfectly well find drawn by Semonides. Alcaeus twice uses βασιλεύς of Zeus (296, 3; 387); he uses τύραννος of Pittacus (348, 3). Much later Aristophanes can speak of Ζῆνα τύραννον (*Nub.* 564), but in early times the distinction between the two terms seems to have been mainta·..ed.

70. D. L. Page, *Class. Rev.* 68, 1954, 106 points out that Semonides 'has the dative in -οισι twenty-six times, but that in -οις here only, and that τοιοῦτος, which occurs six times in this poem, has everywhere else in it a long first vowel, as it has at Archilochus 67, 3. For these reasons, he wishes to delete ll. 69–70.

I see no argument against l. 69, which could well stand even without l. 70. Verdenius pleads that the dialect of Sappho and Alcaeus has τέουτος and that datives in -οις occur in Homer. Neither point is relevant; what the defender of

l. 70 has to do is to produce instances from Ionian iambics. Adequate ones are not forthcoming; at Archilochus 119, 2 μηροῖς may have been followed by a vowel; at 130, 1 and 4 the text is uncertain; and *P.Oxy.* 2325, 2 (*Adesp. Iamb.* 42 West) may not be relevant. That leaves us with l. 74 of our poem, where Arsenius is said to quote ἀστοῖσι⟨ν⟩ for ἀνθρώποις; to a modern ear this may sound offensive after ἄστεος, but we cannot be certain that the ancients felt the same. Certainty is impossible, and shortening of many vowels before other vowels in the same word occurs (see on 57, and cf. fr. 8); but the occurrence in the same line of the unique τοι– and the dangerously isolated dative in -οις obliges us to view l. 70 with some suspicion. Perhaps someone who knew it from another poem wrote it in the margin, and from there it found its way into the text.

The verb ἀγλαΐζομαι occurs in Homer (*Il.* 10, 331; cf. ἐπαγλαΐζομαι at 18, 133), but not in the iambographers or in tragedy; ἀγλαός is found once in Archilochus and (like ἀγλάϊσμα) twice in tragedy.

71.   On the monkey among the Greeks, see Keller 1, 3 f. and W. C. Mac-Dermott, *The Ape in Antiquity*, 1938. As among us, it was proverbial for ugliness; in Archilochus' fable of the fox and the monkey, it seems to have plumed itself on its beauty (see fr. 185–7, especially 187, and cf. Pindar, *Pyth.* 2, 74).

διακριδόν with a superlative occurs at *Il.* 12, 103 and 15, 108.

72.   κακόν: cf. ll. 96 and 115, and also 68.

73.   πρόσωπα in the plural is used of a single person regularly in Homer and occasionally in tragedy (e.g. Sophocles, *El.* 1277, *O.C.* 314).

74.   See on l. 70 above for the problem of the dative in -οις: cf. Archilochus 172, 3–4 νῦν δὲ δὴ πολὺς|ἀστοῖσι φαίνεαι γέλως: Herodotus 3, 29; Sophocles, *O.C.* 902. The ape-woman is the opposite of the orator in *Od.* 8, 173, on whom ἐρχόμενον . . . ἀνὰ ἄστυ θεὸν ὥς εἰσορόωσιν: see Hesiod, *Theog.* 84 f., 91, with West's notes.

75.   ἐπ' αὐχένα βραχεῖα: cf. *Il.* 2, 308 δράκων ἐπὶ νῶτα δαφοινός and *Carm. Pop.* 848, 4–5 Page ἐπὶ γαστέρα λευκά, ἐπὶ νῶτα μέλαινα. But in both these cases the adjective denotes colour; more like is *Il.* 2, 765 ἵππους . . . σταφύληι ἐπὶ νῶτον ἐΐσας. In England a·long neck has been a mark of female beauty at least since the time of King Harold's mistress Edith Swanneck. But in Greek I have found no instances; Marg should not have quoted Bacchylides 13, 84, since ὑψαυχής is not the same as ὑψαύχην.

Commentary

κινεῖται μόγις: the monkey leaps easily from branch to branch, but is an awkward mover on the ground. There is much to be said for placing colons after βραχεῖα and μόγις, but this gives a jerky rhythm, unusual in the poem.

76. 'She has no bottom and is all leg' makes excellent sense. The πυγή was a mark of female beauty in ancient Greece. Hesiod, *Op.* 373 warns against being deceived by a γυνὴ πυγοστόλος: cf. Aristophanes, *Pax* 869b, *Eccl.* 964–5 and see Athenaeus 554c and Alciphron 4, 14 (= 1, 39). G. Säflund, *Aphrodite Kallipygos*, 1964, gives further evidence. ἄπυγος occurs only here, but is restored with much probability by Meineke at Plato Com., fr. 184, 3 Kock; see Dover on Aristophanes, *Nub.* 1014. Verdenius after Koster most appositely quotes Balzac's description of Clotilde de Grandlieu in *Splendeurs et Misères des Courtisanes*, 'Elle était tout jambes'.

Ovid, *Ars Am.* 3, 272 may speak of dry legs as a defect of women; but Haupt's conjecture αὐόκωλος is unnecessary, and does not improve the sense.

ἆ δειλ' is Homeric; ἆ may express contempt, but also pity (see E. Schwentner, *Die primären Interjektionen in den indogermanischen Sprachen*, 1924, 6 f.). M offers the hyperionism ἀτάλης (*sic*): cf. Herodas 3, 35 and 7, 88, and see V. Schmidt, *Sprachliche Untersuchungen zu Herondas*, 1968, 31 f.

77. The verb does not recur before Lycophron 142; note also Meleager 4453 Gow–Page; but παραγκάλισμα and ὑπαγκάλισμα are found in tragedy.

78. δήνεα means 'skills, arts'; they may be ἤπια, as at *Il.* 4, 361, Hesiod, *Theog.* 236, but here the ὀλοφώϊα δήνεα of Circe (*Od.* 10, 289) are more relevant.

τρόποι means 'ways of acting'; the resourceful man knows how to turn himself in various directions as need arises, and is thus πολύτροπος, 'versatile'. The use is not found in Homer or Hesiod, nor in early lyric; at Sappho 68, 7 we cannot tell what τρόπον means. This seems to be the earliest example, despite πολύτροπος in *Od.* 1, 1.

79. ὥσπερ πίθηκος: cf. on l. 37. οὐδὲ . . . μέλει might conceivably mean that the ape-woman has no sense of humour. But it is a great deal likelier that she is indifferent to the ridicule which she is described in ll. 73–4 as exciting. B. van Groningen, *Mnemosyne* 57, 1929, 369 wished to make this clearer by placing l. 79 after l. 74; but they are not very far apart in the transmitted text, and this is hardly necessary. It is disgraceful for a Greek to be indifferent to ridicule; as their

Females of the Species

many words for *Schadenfreude* indicate, the Greeks intensely disliked being the target of the mockery of others. The thought that deters Euripides' Medea from having mercy on her children is that if she does people will laugh at her (404 f.; 1049; cf. 383).

οἱ: P. Maas, *Greek Metre*, s.133 observes that the initial digamma is metrically effective more often in the pronoun of the third person than in any other kind of word.

80.   εὖ ἔρδειν is a common combination in Homer, and in post-Homeric hexameter and elegiac verse the digamma is often effective in it; e.g. at Solon 13, 67; Theognis 105, 573, 955, 1184b, 1263, 1266, 1317. In the early iambographers, this is the only instance.

ὁρᾶν in the sense of 'look to' or 'consider' appears at *Il.* 10, 239 and at Solon 11, 7; ὁρᾶν with ὅπως or with μή meaning 'look to it that' occurs next in Aeschylus (*Eum.* 652; *P.V.* 997). In this, apparently the first instance of the use, the τοῦτο repeated with an effect of emphasis looks forward to the ὅπως clause.

82.   West prints τι κῶς, which is certainly close to what is transmitted; but the point is that she tries to do harm to someone else (cf. 1. 80), and Meineke by changing one letter gives just the sense we should expect.

ἔρξειεν: the optative stands, although the sequence is primary, presumably because the mood of the verb is influenced by the optative in l. 80; thus Wackernagel, *Vorlesungen zur Syntax* I, 58. κακὸν ἔρδειν τινα is common; cf., e.g., Hesiod, *Op.* 327.

83.   For the Greeks as for us, the busy bee was proverbial; see Keller II, 421 f. and H. K. Ransome, *The Sacred Bee*, 1937. Hesiod contrasts drones with workers, comparing women with the former (*Theog.* 594 f.; cf. *Op.* 303 f.); the insufferable Ischomachus in Xenophon's *Oeconomicus* (7, 17) compares the wife in charge of a household to a queen bee.

τήν τις εὐτυχεῖ λαβών: Verdenius seems to me to read rather too much into εὐτυχεῖ when he says it underlines the element of pure luck in getting a good wife.

84.   προσιζάνει implies the metaphor of an insect settling on a flower; (cf. Aeschylus, *P.V.* 275–6 . . . πλανωμένη|πρὸς ἄλλοτ' ἄλλον πημονὴ προσιζάνει); doubtless the metaphor was suggested to the poet by the subject-matter.

Commentary

The god Momos is mentioned by Hesiod, *Theog.* 214; according to the *Cypria* (fr. 1 Allen p. 117 = fr. 1 Bethe p. 6) he advised Zeus to solve the earth's population problem by begetting a beautiful daughter whom men could fight over; in Aesop (Hausrath 1, 128) he blames Zeus for not putting the bull's eyes on its horns, Prometheus for not making a man's mental processes visible (cf. Euripides, *Medea* 516 f.) and Athena for not having made the first house on wheels, so that its occupants could get away from bad neighbours. The noun occurs in Homer only at *Od.* 2, 86 μῶμον ἀνάψαι. It is found in Pindar and Bacchylides, but is rare in tragedy—personification may account for its presence at Sophocles, fr. 257[1]— which prefers μομφή. Here the poet seems to imagine Momos flying about from person to person, like a distasteful insect.

85–6.   A. W. Gomme in the article in which he argued that women in Athens in the fifth and fourth centuries were not so badly off as had been commonly assumed pointed out that even this misogynistic poem contained this striking testimony to true marital affection (*Essays in Greek History and Literature*, 1937, 98, n. 1; the article first appeared in *Classical Philology* 20, 1925). Gomme quotes Plato, *Laws* 840D ὅταν δ' εἰς τοῦτο ἡλικίας ἔλθωσι, συνδυασθέντες ἄρρην θηλείαι κατὰ χάριν καὶ θήλεια ἄρρενι, τὸν λοιπὸν χρόνον ὁσίως καὶ δικαίως ζῶσιν ἐμμένοντες βεβαίως ταῖς πρώταις τῆς φιλίας ὁμολογίαις: he also draws attention to Aristotle, *Eth. Nic.* 1162a16–29 (on the natural affinity between man and woman) and Plutarch, *Solon* 20 (see also *Amatorius* 769A f., translated by D. A. Russell, *Plutarch*, 1973, 92); had it then been known, he might have quoted the words of a young husband in a comedy, probably by Menander (P. Antinoop. 15, 11–12, on p. 327 of F. H. Sandbach's Oxford text of Menander; for commentary see J. W. B. Barns and H. Lloyd-Jones, *Journal of Hellenic Studies* 84, 1964, 21 f.):

> αὐτῆς ἐλευθέρωι γὰρ ἤθει καὶ βίωι
> δεθεὶς ἀπλάστωι τὴν φιλοῦσαν ἠγάπων.

For the anaphora cf. Pindar, *Pyth.* 10, 66 φιλέων φιλέοντ', ἄγων ἄγοντα προφρόνως. φίλη, of course, is active in sense.

85.   The idea that one of a wife's main duties, if not her principal duty, was to increase her husband's wealth by the skilful management of his household was widely prevalent in ancient Greece; the locus classicus is Xenophon, *Oeconomicus*

---

[1] We know nothing of the plot of Sophocles' satyr play *Momos.*

85

7, 10 f., on which see J. K. Anderson, *Xenophon*, 1974, 175 f. βίος here means 'substance'; θάλλει is a metaphor from plants; for ἐπαέξεται cf. *Od.* 14, 65–6 θεὸς δ' ἐπὶ ἔργον ἀέξηι.

87. ὀνομάκλυτος is an exalted word, in keeping with the elevated tone of this passage; cf. *Il.* 22, 51 and *Hymn. Merc.* 59. On the contraction, see V. Schmidt, *Sprachliche Untersuchungen ʒu Herondas*, 1968, 7, with n. 22.

88. ἀριπρεπής is a heroic word; at *Il.* 6, 476 f. Hector prays that his son may be ἀριπρεπέα Τρώεσσιν. But here the meaning is not that all women will know of her, but that she will be eminent among all women; cf. *Il.* 2, 483 ἐκπρεπέ' ἐν πολλοῖσι καὶ ἔξοχον ἡρώεσσιν, and Luke 1, 42 εὐλογημένη σὺ ἐν γυναιξίν.

89. θεῖος is an epithet of men in Homer, but less often in tragedy (see Fraenkel on Aeschylus, *Ag.* 1547); in general, see L. Bieler, Θεῖος ἀνήρ I, 1935, 9 f.; II 1936, 41 f. More rarely it is applied to things; e.g. at *Od.* 2, 341 and 9, 205 θεῖον ποτόν. χάρις may shine from a man (e.g. *Il.* 14, 183 χάρις δ' ἀπελάμπετο πολλή and *Od.* 6, 237 κάλλεϊ καὶ χάρισι στίλβων); a god may pour it over him, as Athene does over Telemachus (*Od.* 2, 12 θεσπεσίην δ' ἄρα τῶι γε χάριν κατέχευεν 'Αθήνη. For a Homeric reduplicated perfect used of a pervasive glow, cf. *Od.* 6, 45 λευκὴ δ' ἐπιδέδρομεν αἴγλη, and Sappho 31, 9–10 says λέπτον δ' αὔτικα χρῶι πῦρ ὑπαδεδρόμηκεν: the form ἀμφιδέδρομεν occurs in Archilochus 37.

90–1. The bee's σωφροσύνη was proverbial; according to Aelian, *De Anim.* 5, 11 they are so prudish that they attack people who use scent; cf. Plutarch, *Praecepta Conjugalia* 44 = 144D.

This picture of what went on among women when they were alone recalls assertions in comedy that the older women corrupted the younger ones; cf. Menander, *Dysc.* 384 f., where Sostratus says how lucky it is that the girl he has fallen in love with has been brought up by her father, and not exposed to the influence of a grandmother or a nurse; cf. Antiphanes, *Misoponeros* 159 Kock (cited by Handley ad loc.). Women were often left in the company of women slaves, who are imagined in literature as being like the nurse in the *Hippolytus* or Gyllis in the first poem of Herodas.

91. Cf. Plato Comicus, fr. 2 Demianczuk ἀφροδίσιος λόγος.

Commentary

93. πολυφραδής recurs only at Hesiod, *Theog.* 494; cf. fr. 310 πολυφραδέοντα. Here ends the first part of the poem.

94–5. This must refer to the women of the first nine types; one might expect ἐκεῖνα rather than ταῦτα, since ἄλλα shows that the bee-woman is not referred to, but the sense is clear, and emendation is not needed. Verdenius may be right in taking παρ' ἀνδράσιν with both verbs, which makes perfectly good grammar (he quotes several examples, like Aeschylus, *P.V.* 21 οὔτε φωνὴν οὔτε του μορφὴν βροτῶν) but the meaning may be 'exist and remain with men'. I see no particular advantage in taking μένει as future rather than present; the man cannot expel them, because Zeus has arranged things so that men cannot do without them.

96. τοῦτο is predicative and strongly emphatic; κακόν is not the predicate; the train of thought must be, '(men would get rid of them else); for this is the greatest plague Zeus has made—women'. The sentence echoes 72 (cf. 93), and recurs at 115; it expresses the theme of the poem, and resounds throughout it like a remorseless drumbeat. It has reminded G. E. R. Lloyd, *Polarity and Analogy*, 1966, 42 with n. 4, of dark cultures which make the female element the source of all evil.

98. Cf. 68. The MSS. have τωι or τω, which is best interpreted as τῶι, 'for him'; τωι (= τινι), which Verdenius thinks not impossible, would be feeble. Koeler's τοι, with comma at the end of l. 97, makes sense but hardly improves on τῶι.

99. Cf. Alcman 1, 37 ὁ δ' ὄλβιος ὅστις εὔφρων|ἁμέραν [δι]απλέκει ἄκλαυτος. There as here it means 'cheerful' (see Page, *Alcman: The Partheneion*, 1951, 83). In both places we find not ἄπαντα χρόνον, but ἄπασαν ἡμέραν: man is ἐφήμερος, a creature of the day, a concept explained by Hermann Fränkel in a justly famous article ('Man's ἐφήμερος nature according to Pindar and others', in *TAPA* 77, 1946, 131 f.; German version in *Wege und Formen frühgriechischen Denkens*, 2nd edn., 1960, 23 f.).

100. πέλεται is corrupt; the early editors' idea that a metrical lengthening of the lambda is possible has no substance. No attempt at emendation carries conviction; Verdenius lists some poor specimens, and adds another. I do not understand the favour shown to Ahrens' τέλλεται, which would mean 'come into being';

Bergk's γίνεται at least makes sense, but colourless sense, and fails to explain the corruption. If I had to guess at it, I should guess ναιετᾶι, considered by Wilhelm, *Symbolae Osloenses* 27, 1949, 51 but rejected by him. Hesiod, *Theog.* 592 calls women πῆμα μέγα θνητοῖσι, μετ' ἀνδράσι ναιετάουσαι.

101.   αἶψα: cf. *Od.* 3, 147 οὐ γάρ τ' αἶψα θεῶν τρέπεται νόος αἰὲν ἐόντων: for the notion, cf. *Od.* 1, 270 ὅππως κε μνηστῆρας ἀπώσεαι ἐκ μεγάροιο. The allegorical personification of Famine is as early as Hesiod; cf. *Op.* 299, where Perses is urged to work ὄφρα σε Λιμὸς |ἐχθαίρηι, φιλέηι δέ σ' ἐυστέφανος Δημήτηρ. Radermacher quotes from an inscription from Termessus (103) δίωξε γὰρ εἰς ἅλα Λιμόν and Zenobius 4, 93 says that at Athens during a famine a piece of land was dedicated to Λιμός. An unwelcome δαίμων is called an unpleasant housemate also by Aeschylus, *Suppl.* 415 τὸν πανώλεθρον θεόν|βαρὺν ξύνοικον θησόμεσθ' ἀλάστορα and *Ag.* 1641 ὁ δυσφιλὴς σκότωι|λιμὸς ξύνοικος μαλθακόν σφ' ἐπόψεται and by Sappho 148, 1 ὁ πλοῦτος ἄνευθ' ἀρέτας|οὐκ ἀσίνης πάροικος. West keeps θεῶν. He could argue that the house of Hades is hateful even to the gods (*Il.* 20, 65); that the Aeschylean Apollo calls the Erinyes στύγη θεῶν (*Eum.* 644; cf. 73, 191, etc.); and that the chorus of the *O.T.* of Sophocles calls Ares τὸν ἀπότιμον ἐν θεοῖς θεόν (215). But is Famine an enemy of the gods? Of mortals, rather; cf. Aeschylus, *Sept.* 721, where the Chorus calls the Erinys θεὸν οὐ θεοῖς ὁμοίαν (on the punctuation, see Fraenkel, *Kleine Beiträge zur klassischen Philologie*, 1964, 399 f.); and an ancient commentator writes θεοὶ γὰρ δωτῆρες ἐάων. He has rightly seen that the phrase is a kind of oxymoron; his comment here might be οἱ δὲ θεοὶ εὐμενεῖς. I follow Grotius in writing θεόν. Thus Iocaste says of Adikia at Euripides, *Phoen.* 532 ἄδικος ἡ θεός.

103.   δοκῆι with the infinitive here means 'to have a mind to', as at Aeschylus, *Ag.* 16 ὅταν δ' ἀείδειν ἢ μινύρεσθαι δοκῶ. θυμηδεῖν means 'to enjoy himself', i.e. 'to feast'; in Callimachus, fr. 227, 4 θυμηδία occurs in the description of an all-night festival, and Verdenius compares Eupolis, fr. 161 Kock, where the context is similar.

104.   Wilamowitz, *Der Glaube der Hellenen* 1, 1931, 359, n. 4 thinks that the alternatives number three: 'at home, without a special reason, or on the occasion of a sacrifice, when he gets a portion (μοῖρα) of the meal offered to the god, or when someone has invited him.' With Marg and Verdenius, I take κατ' οἶκον to apply to both the alternatives introduced by ἤ, so that the alternatives number not

three but two. θεοῦ μοῖραν could indeed refer to a sacrificial portion; but in this context, where it is parallel with ἀνθρώπου χάριν, it is surely likelier that it means 'by the favour of a god'. When a god does one a kindness, it is a μοῖρα: when a man does it, it is a χάρις. Marg quotes Aristophanes, *Pax* 1143 ἐμπιεῖν ἔμοιγ' ἀρέσκει τοῦ θεοῦ δρῶντος καλῶς: when a god has granted one good fortune, ὅταν θεοῦ μοῖρα πέμπηι ... ὄλβον (Pindar, *Ol.* 2, 21), it is proper to enjoy oneself.

105. μῶμον: see on 84.

κορύσσομαι, from κόρυς, a helmet, is a Homeric verb used of heroes arming themselves for battle, and applied metaphorically to waves raising their heads. For a hearer accustomed to such expressions as Αἴας δὲ κορύσσετο νώροπι χαλκῶι (*Il.* 7, 206), it most effectively describes the wife's aggressiveness. Not unlike is [Hesiod], *Aspis* 198 μάχην ἐθέλουσα κορύσσειν.

106. In Greek of this date the law discovered by J. Wackernagel, *Indoger-manische Forschungen* 1, 1892, 319 f. = *Kleine Schriften* 1 f., according to which postpositives stand in second place in the sentence, is strictly observed. The only instances of delayed γάρ earlier than this listed by Denniston, *GP* 97 are *Il.* 17, 363 οὐδ' οἳ γάρ and 21, 331 ἄντα σέθεν γάρ: we are a long way from the postpone-ment of γάρ to as late as seventh word in the sentence which Menander employs, perhaps in imitation of colloquial speech (Wilamowitz, *Menander: Das Schieds-gericht*, 156). The placing of γυνὴ at this point surely lends it strong emphasis: 'where there is a *woman*'.

107. ξεῖνον together with μολόντα seems to indicate a visitor who has come from a distance, and οὐδὲ to imply 'still less could they invite a neighbour'.

For προφρόνως used of entertainment, cf., e.g., *Il.* 6, 173 προφρονέως μιν τῖεν: πρόφρων δέχομαι occurs at *Il.* 23, 647.

The subject of δεκοίατο is a vaguely understood 'they', meaning 'the other men' or 'the members of the household'. One would expect δέκοιτό τις, but this can hardly have been corrupted to a form with the correct Ionic ending of the third person plural of the optative. Potential optatives without ἄν are fairly common in epic (W. W. Goodwin, *Greek Moods and Tenses*, 80–1; Kühner-Gerth 1, 225 f.; W. S. Barrett, *Euripides, Hippolytos*, 379–80); in tragedy, it is admitted in certain types of utterance (see Barrett, l.c., and Fraenkel, *Aeschylus, Agamem-non*, 620, n. 2). I can find no other instance in the early iambographers; but we have so little material that this may be due to accident. Meineke inserted ἄν after μολόντ'.

108.   τοι gives the effect of pointing a finger at the person addressed; see Denniston, *GP* 537 f. It is rare in the early iambographers; but cf. Archilochus fr. 13, 14; 144, 1; *Adesp. Iamb.* 35, 9. There is no need to adopt Hermann's conjecture τωι, which gives a weaker sense. σωφρονεῖν often implies 'chaste' or 'respectable', as at Aeschylus, *Cho.* 140 and Euripides, *Bacch.* 314.

109.   λωβωμένη is an extremely strong word, used in Homer of mutilation or of deadly insult; τυγχάνει λ. means 'in the event does the greatest outrage'.

110.   It is conceivable that the text is corrupt, as some have thought. But it is a great deal more probable that the poet has here employed aposiopesis, the device of breaking off a sentence to secure a particular effect. Bergk pointed out that this is particularly common when sexual matters are in question. On aposiopesis in general, see G. Gerber, *Die Sprache als Kunst* II, 1885 (reprinted 1961), 272 f. For aposiopesis of this type, cf. Sophocles, *O.T.* 1288 f. τὸν πατροκτόνον,|τὸν μητρὸς αὐδῶν ἀνόσι' οὐδὲ ῥητά μοι: Aristophanes, *Vesp.* 1178 ἔπειτα δ' ὡς ὁ Καρδοπίων τὴν μητέρα—: Callimachus, fr. 75, 4 Ἥρην γάρ κοτέ φασι—: Theocritus 1, 105 with Gow's note: Virgil, *Ecl.* 3, 8 novimus et qui te, transversa tuentibus hircis.
    κεχηνότος: for this verb denoting inattention, cf. Aristophanes, *Eq.* 1032 ὅταν σύ ποι ἄλλοσε χάσκηις; on the use of this verb in comedy, see J. Taillardat, *Les Images d'Aristophane*, 1962, 264 f.
    Verdenius tries to avoid assuming an aposiopesis; the only passage he alleges to be parallel is Plato, *Symp.* 220B, where a long series of genitive absolutes is followed by οὗτος δέ. That is hardly relevant to a case in which there is only one genitive absolute, as here. Denniston, *GP* 181 (bottom) observes that δέ following a participial clause seems to be confined to prose; the only possible exceptions he notes are this passage and Euripides, *Hypsipyle* fr. 60, 11, on which see G. W. Bond on p. 104 of his edition of the play (1963).

110–11.   Hesiod, *Op.* 701 warns his farmer to be circumspect in choosing a wife, μὴ γείτοσι χάρματα γήμηις: but the pleasure he has in mind is not mere *Schadenfreude.* The καί implies that the newest victim is only one of a long succession. καί often follows a sentence enunciating a general principle and begins one that illustrates it by giving a particular instance; cf. e.g., *Od.* 21, 295, where a warning against the dangers of getting drunk is followed by οἶνος καὶ Κένταυρον . . . ἄασε; Sophocles, *Ant.* 944 f.; Theocritus 7, 149 with Gow's note.

ἁμαρτάνειν is rare in the early iambographers; perhaps this will encourage a certain kind of scholar to argue that they lack a sense of guilt. At *Adesp. Iamb.* 35, 11 it means 'to do wrong'; but at Hipponax 121, as here, it means 'to be mistaken'.

112–14. These lines together amount to a variant upon a common gnome, whose basic element is tersely expressed in Menander, fr. 521 οὐδεὶς ἐφ' αὑτοῦ τὰ κακὰ συνορᾷ, Πάμφιλε,|σαφῶς, ἑτέρου δ' ἀσχημονοῦντος ὄψεται and at Catullus 22, 21 non videmus manticae quod in tergo est (with allusion to an Aesopic fable told by Phaedrus 4, 10 and Babrius 66).

112. This is the only instance of ὅς = suus in the early iambographers. But in a style so permeated with Homerisms it is hardly surprising; it is found in Pindar, and even in tragedy.

αἰνέσει μεμνημένος here means 'will take care to praise', 'will do all he can to praise'; cf. *Il.* 19, 153 ὧδέ τις ὑμείων μεμνημένος ἀνδρὰ μαχέσθω: Hesiod, *Op.* 422 τῆμος ἄρ' ὑλοτομεῖν μεμνημένος ὥρια ἔργα.

113. μωμήσεται: see on 84. The verb occurs in Homer (*Il.* 3, 412), Theognis, Simonides and occasionally in tragedy and comedy; but the dramatists prefer μέμψομαι.

115. See on 96.

116. πέδη(ι) codd.: Koeler emended to πέδης (Meineke ἀρρήκτου πέδης), Crusius to πέδην, and it is not easy to decide between them. The wording recalls *Il.* 15, 19 f. περὶ χερσὶ δὲ δεσμὸν ἴηλα| . . . ἄρρηκτον: 13, 36 f. ἀμφὶ δὲ ποσσὶ πέδας ἔβαλε χρυσείας,|ἀρρήκτους ἀλύτους and it reminds us of accounts of the binding of Prometheus, like Hesiod, *Theog.* 521 f. δῆσε δ' ἀλυκτοπέδῃσι and Aeschylus, *P.V.* 6 ἀδαμαντίνων δεσμῶν ἐν ἀρρήκτοις πέδαις. I slightly incline to prefer πέδην: if πέδης is right, then Meineke's ἀρρήκτου is probably right also. On erotic Ἀνάγκη, see H. Schreckenberg, *Ananke*, 1964, 59 f.

117.   τε may be used to give a causal colour to a relative; and that has encouraged people who have wished to show that the poem was complete. But an unbiased reader must surely admit that he takes τε here to mean 'and', and that after the poet has said, 'Since when some have died fighting for a woman', he expects him to continue with 'And others . . .' Even if one could accept τε here as a mere adjunct to the relative, the end would be impossibly abrupt. We must accept that the poem is not complete; how much more there was is impossible to say, but the poet may have added a number of mythological examples.

'Αΐδης (- ∪-) is regular in Ionic; see V. Schmidt, *Sprachliche Untersuchangem zu Herondas*, 1968, 1 f.

118.   It was a commonplace that those who died at Troy died for Helen; see, e.g., *Il.* 2, 161–2 (= 177–8) 'Αργείην 'Ελένην, ἧς εἵνεκα πολλοὶ 'Αχαιῶν|ἐν Τροίηι ἀπόλοντο: Hesiod, *Op.* 165: Aeschylus, *Ag.* 62, 448, 800, 1455–7.

ἀμφιδηριᾶσθαι does not occur again before Lycophron 1437, but the simple verb is Homeric.

Fr. 6 of Semonides:

> γυναικὸς οὐδὲν χρῆμ' ἀνὴρ ληΐζεται
> ἐσθλῆς ἄμεινον οὐδὲ ῥίγιον κακῆς

'a man wins no prize better than a good woman or horrider than a bad one' must echo Hesiod, *Op.* 702–3.

> οὐ μὲν γάρ τι γυναικὸς ἀνὴρ ληΐζετ' ἄμεινον
> τῆς ἀγαθῆς, τῆς δ' αὖτε κακῆς οὐ ῥίγιον ἄλλο

'for a man wins no prize better than the good woman, nor any horrider than the bad one'.

The occurrence in both passages of such comparatively unusual words as ληΐζομαι, properly used of capturing booty, and ῥίγιον, 'horrider', leaves little room for doubt; compare the imitation of Hesiod, *Op.* 582 f. by Alcaeus 347 (a). It has been suggested that this fragment comes from the missing part of our poem; but I agree with Verdenius that its tone seems too favourable towards women for this to seem very likely. More probably it came from another poem whose mood was less misogynistic.

Appendixes

APPENDIX I

Other Fragments of Semonides

The most substantial fragment of Semonides after the poem on women is fr. 1 (in West's *Iambi et Elegi Graeci* II, p. 96):

> ὦ παῖ, τέλος μὲν Ζεὺς ἔχει βαρύκτυπος
> πάντων ὅσ᾽ ἐστὶ καὶ τίθησ᾽ ὅκηι θέλει,
> νοῦς δ᾽ οὐκ ἐπ᾽ ἀνθρώποισιν, ἀλλ᾽ ἐπήμεροι
> ἃ δὴ βοτὰ ζόουσιν, οὐδὲν εἰδότες
> 5   ὅκως ἕκαστον ἐκτελευτήσει θεός.
> ἐλπὶς δὲ πάντας κἀπιπειθείη τρέφει
> ἄπρηκτον ὁρμαίνοντας· οἱ μὲν ἡμέρην
> μένουσιν ἐλθεῖν, οἱ δ᾽ ἐτέων περιτροπάς·
> νέωτα δ᾽ οὐδεὶς ὅστις οὐ δοκεῖ βροτῶν
> 10   Πλούτωι τε κἀγαθοῖσιν ἵξεσθαι φίλος.
> φθάνει δὲ τὸν μὲν γῆρας ἄζηλον λαβὸν
> πρὶν τέρμ᾽ ἵκηται, τοὺς δὲ δύστηνοι βροτῶν
> φθείρουσι νοῦσοι, τοὺς δ᾽ Ἄρει δεδμημένους
> πέμπει μελαίνης Ἀΐδης ὑπὸ χθονός·
> 15   οἱ δ᾽ ἐν θαλάσσηι λαίλαπι κλονεόμενοι
> καὶ κύμασιν πολλοῖσι πορφυρῆς ἁλὸς
> θνήσκουσιν, εὖτ᾽ ἂν μὴ δυνήσωνται ζόειν·
> οἱ δ᾽ ἀγχόνην ἄψαντο δυστήνωι μόρωι
> καὐτάγρετοι λείπουσιν ἡλίου φάος.
> 20   οὕτω κακῶν ἄπ᾽ οὐδέν, ἀλλὰ μυρίαι
> βροτοῖσι κῆρες κἀνεπίφραστοι δύαι
> καὶ πήματ᾽ ἐστίν. εἰ δ᾽ ἐμοὶ πιθοίατο,
> οὐκ ἂν κακῶν ἐρῶιμεν, οὐδ᾽ ἐπ᾽ ἄλγεσιν
> κακοῖς ἔχοντες θυμὸν αἰκιζοίμεθα.

'Boy, power in all the things that there are belongs to loud-thundering Zeus, and he disposes them as he wishes. And intelligence does not belong to men; no, the creatures of a day live like cattle, with no knowledge of how the god will bring each thing to an end. Hope and persuasion sustain them all as they pursue their futile impulses; some wait for next day to come, and some for the day a year ahead, and every single mortal thinks that next year he will become friends with wealth and with luxury. But one is seized on by odious old age before he reaches his term; other mortals are destroyed by miserable maladies; others are brought low by the war-god and taken by Hades under the black earth. Others die at sea, battered by the gale and the dark sea's many waves, after having failed to earn a living; and others fasten a noose and meet a miserable end, leaving the sun's light by their own act. So no calamity is spared them; no, mortals have ten thousand spirits of death and sorrows and disasters that come unseen. If they took my advice, we should not long for what destroys us, nor torture ourselves by enduring cruel pains.'

Many scholars have assigned to Semonides a third substantial fragment, which West, op. cit., prints as fr. 8 of Simonides, though he doubts Simonidean authorship:

> ἓν δὲ τὸ κάλλιστον Χῖος ἔειπεν ἀνήρ·
> "οἵη περ φύλλων γενεή, τοίη δὲ καὶ ἀνδρῶν"·
> παῦροί μιν θνητῶν οὔασι δεξάμενοι
> στέρνοις ἐγκατέθεντο· πάρεστι γὰρ ἐλπὶς ἑκάστωι
> 5   ἀνδρῶν, ἥ τε νέων στήθεσιν ἐμφύεται.
> θνητῶν δ' ὄφρά τις ἄνθος ἔχηι πολυήρατον ἥβης,
> κοῦφον ἔχων θυμὸν πόλλ' ἀτέλεστα νοεῖ·
> οὔτε γὰρ ἐλπίδ' ἔχει γηρασέμεν οὔτε θανεῖσθαι,
> οὐδ', ὑγιὴς ὅταν ἦι, φροντίδ' ἔχει καμάτου.
> 10   νήπιοι, οἷς ταύτηι κεῖται νόος, οὐδὲ ἴσασιν
> ὡς χρόνος ἔσθ' ἥβης καὶ βιότου ὀλίγος
> θνητοῖς. ἀλλὰ σὺ ταῦτα μαθὼν βιότου ποτὶ τέρμα
> ψυχῆι τῶν ἀγαθῶν τλῆθι χαριζόμενος.

'The finest thing the man of Chios [Homer] ever said was this: "Like the life of leaves, such is the life of men." Few among mortals have taken it in with their ears and stored it in their hearts; because each man is attended by Hope, which grows in the chests of young men. And so long as a mortal has the delightful bloom of youth, he thinks many futile thoughts in his light-heartedness; because he never imagines that he will grow old or die, and while he is well he never thinks of sickness. They whose minds lie in this direction are foolish, and they do not

96

Appendix I

realise that the time of youth and life is short for mortals. So understand this, and as you approach the end of life bear up, and indulge yourself with luxuries.'

Stobaeus, who preserves the piece, ascribes it to Simonides. We have seen (above, p. 15) that iambic verse attributed to Simonides is to be given to Semonides; but this fragment is in elegiac metre. Yet in modern times it has usually been credited to the Amorgine; Bergk's ascription to him was accepted by Wilamowitz, Maas and Schadewaldt, as well as by Schmid and Lesky in their histories of Greek literature; Werner Jaeger in *Paideia* I 448, n. 57 (English edition) goes so far as to call it 'one of the most certain results of philological research'.[1] Those who have believed in it have done so, for the most part, because of what they feel to be a remarkable coincidence between the attitude expressed in it and that expressed in fr. 1 of Semonides. Lately their case has been eloquently put by Daniel Babut in a learned article.[2] He argues that both poems are marked out from Homer by the hedonistic attitude to which their pessimistic view of human prospects leads them, which in his opinion has much in common with the hedonistic attitude of Mimnermus.

Those who have resisted the attribution to Semonides have done so, for the most part, because they thought the style pointed to a later date; O. Crusius' remarks of 1894 have been taken up in recent times by Hermann Fränkel and by Martin West.[3] Whether or not the verses could have been written as early as the seventh century is not easy to decide, there being relatively little elegiac verse of that period. Yet the outlook upon human life expressed in the two poems is one so widely diffused among the Greek poets of the seventh, sixth and even fifth centuries that we should be wary of allowing the similarity of content to persuade us that they come from the same hand. Many sepulchral epigrams were attributed to Simonides, and as Fränkel says the verses might well come from one of these. So far as we know, no elegiac verse by Semonides has come down to us.

---

[1] Wilamowitz, *Homerische Untersuchungen*, 1884, 352; *Textgeschichte der griechischen Lyriker*, 1900, 58, n. 1; *Sappho und Simonides*, 1913, 273 f.; Maas, *R.–E.* III A, 1934, 185; Schadewaldt, *Die Antike* 9, 1933, 294; Schmid-Stählin, I i 1929, 397, n.8; Lesky, *History of Greek Literature* (English edition, 1966), p. 114; Jaeger, *Paidea* I (English edition 1939), p. 448, n. 57.

[2] *Revue des Etudes Grecques* 84, 1971, 17 f.; see the bibliography of the problem on p. 23, n. 36.

[3] O. Crusius, *Philologus* 54, 1894, 715, n. 15; Fränkel, *Dichtung und Philosophie des frühgriechischen Altertums*, 2nd edn., 1962, p. 237, n. 14; West, *Iambi et Elegi Graeci*, 1972, ii p. 114, and *SGEI*, 180: see Babut, loc. cit.

APPENDIX II

A Fragment of Phocylides

Phocylides fr. 2 Diehl

> καὶ τόδε Φωκυλίδεω· τετόρων ἀπὸ τῶνδε γένοντο
> φῦλα γυναικείων· ἢ μὲν κυνός, ἢ δὲ μελίσσης,
> ἢ δὲ συὸς βλοσυρῆς, ἢ δ᾽ ἵππου χαιτηέσσης.
> εὔφορος ἥδε, ταχεῖα, περίδρομος, εἶδος ἀρίστη·
> ἡ δὲ συὸς βλοσυρῆς οὔτ᾽ ἂρ κακὴ οὐδὲ μὲν ἐσθλή·
> ἡ δὲ κυνὸς χαλεπή τε καὶ ἄγριος· ἡ δὲ μελίσσης
> οἰκονόμος τ᾽ ἀγαθὴ καὶ ἐπίσταται ἐργάζεσθαι·
> ἧς εὔχευ, φίλ᾽ ἑταῖρε, λαχεῖν γάμου ἱμερόεντος.

'This too is by Phocylides. The tribes of women originated from these four creatures: one from a bitch, one from a bee, one from a bristled sow, one from a mare with a long mane. The last is graceful, speedy, a runabout, a beauty. The one from the bristled sow is neither bad nor good. The one from the bitch is cross and savage. The one from the bee is a good housekeeper and knows how to work. Pray, dear friend, to get *her* in delightful marriage.'

The New Archilochus Fragment

Professor R. Merkelbach of Cologne and Dr. M. L. West, Fellow of University College, Oxford, and Professor-elect of Greek at Bedford College, London, have lately published (in *Zeitschrift für Papyrologie und Epigraphik* 14, 1974, 97 f.) a remarkable new fragment of an epode of Archilochus from a papyrus in the Cologne collection. With great kindness they have allowed me to reproduce their text, and my colleague Professor Martin Robertson has kindly permitted me to print his translation (which first appeared in *Arion*).

The fragment begins in the middle of a conversation between the poet and a young girl. It seems certain that she is the sister of Neobule (mentioned in l. 16), and therefore the younger of the two daughters of Lycambes whom Archilochus is said to have wooed without success. Amphimedo (l. 7) was presumably Lycambes' wife.

Merkelbach (p. 113) seems to think that the poet deprived the girl of her virginity. But to me it seems clear that what is described is *ejaculatio praecox* (note ll. 9–10, 15–16; this was a common method of birth-control). B. Marzullo, *Nuova Antologia* 2081, 1974, 3f. and T. Gelzer, whose article is not yet published, think the piece is Hellenistic; their only serious argument, that verse-end occurs at the end of each of the three kola of the dimeter, is not decisive.

ἀπο
πάμπαν ἀνασχόμενος ἶσον δέ τολμ[
εἰ δ' ὦν ἐπείγεαι καί σε θυμὸς ἰθύει[,
ἔστιν ἐν ἡμετέρου ἣ νῦν μέγ' ἱμείρε[ι γάμου
καλὴ τέρεινα παρθένος. δοκέω δέ μι[ν
εἶδος ἄμωμον ἔχειν. τὴν δὴ σὺ πένθ[
τοσαῦτ' ἐφώνει. τὴν δ' ἐγὼ ἀνταμει[βόμην.
"Ἀμφιμεδοῦς θύγατερ ἐσθλῆς τε καὶ [
γυναικός, ἣν νῦν γῆ κατ' εὐρώεσσ' ἔ[χει,
τ]έρψιές εἰσι θεῆς πολλαὶ νέοισιν ἀνδ[ράσιν
παρὲξ τὸ θεῖον χρῆμα. τῶν τις ἀρκέσε[ι.
τ]αῦτα δ' ἐφ' ἡσυχίης εὖτ' ἄν μελάνθη[
ἐ]γώ τε καὶ σὺ σὺν θεῶι βουλεύσομεν.
π]είσομαι ὥς με κέλεαι. πολλόν μ' ἐ[
θρ]ιγκοῦ δ' ἔνερθε καὶ πυλέων ὑποθ[
μ]ή τι μέγαιρε φίλη. σχήσω γὰρ ἐς ποη[φόρους
κ]ήπους. τὸ δὴ νῦν γνῶθι. Νεοβούλη[ν μὲν ὦν
ἄ]λλος ἀνὴρ ἐχέτω. αἰαῖ πέπειρα δ.[
ἄν]θος δ' ἀπερρύηκε παρθενήϊον
κ]αὶ χάρις ἣ πρὶν ἐπῆν. κόρον γὰρ οὐ κ[άτεσχέ πω,
. .]ης δὲ μέτρ' ἔφηνε μαινόλις γυνή.
ἐς] κόρακας ἄπεχε. μὴ τοῦτο ε̣φ̣ ι̣τ̣α̣ν̣[
ὅ]πως ἐγὼ γυναῖκα τ[ο]ιαύτην ἔχων
γεί]τοσι χάρμ' ἔσομαι. πολλὸν σὲ βούλο[μαι πάρος.
σὺ] μὲν γὰρ οὔτ' ἄπιστος οὔτε διπλόη,
ἡ δ]ὲ μάλ' ὀξυτέρη, πολλοὺς δὲ ποιεῖτα[ι φίλους.
δέ]δοιχ' ὅπως μὴ τυφλὰ κἀλιτήμερα
σπ]ουδῆι ἐπειγόμενος τὼς ὥσπερ ἡ κ[ύων τέκω."
τοσ]αῦτ' ἐφώνεον. παρθένον δ' ἐν ἄνθε[σιν
τηλ]εθάεσσι λαβὼν ἔκλινα. μαλθακῆι δ[έ μιν
χλαί]νηι καλύψας, αὐχέν' ἀγκάλῃς ἔχω[ν,
. . .]ματι παυ[σ]αμένην τὼς ὥστε νέβρ[
μαζ]ῶν τε χερσὶν ἠπίως ἐφηψάμην
. . .] . έφηνε νέον ἥβης ἐπήλυ̣σ̣ιν χρόα̣[.
ἅπαν τ]ε σῶμα καλὸν ἀμφαφώμενος
. . . .]ον ἀφῆκα μένος, ξανθῆς ἐπιψαύ[ων τριχός.

Appendix III

'. . . but if you're in a hurry and can't wait for me
there's another girl in our house who's quite ready
to marry, a pretty girl, just right for you.'
That was what she said, but I can talk too.
'Daughter of dear Amphimedo,' I said,
'(a fine woman she was—pity she's dead)
there are plenty of kinds of pretty play
young men and girls can know and not go all the way
—something like that will do. As for marrying,
we'll talk about that again when your mourning
is folded away, god willing. But now
I'll be good, I promise—I do know how.
Don't be hard, darling. Truly I'll stay
out on the garden-grass, not force the doorway
—just try. But as for that sister of yours,
someone else can have her. The bloom's gone—she's coarse
—the charm too (she had it)—now she's on heat
the whole time, can't keep away from it—
damn her, don't let anyone saddle me with that.
With a wife like she is I shouldn't half
give the nice neighbours a belly-laugh.
You're all right, darling. You're simple and straight
—she takes her meat off anyone's plate.
I'ld be afraid if I married her
my children would be like the bitch's litter
—born blind, and several months too early.'
But I'd talked enough. I laid the girl
down among the flowers. A soft cloak spread,
my arm round her neck, I comforted
her fear. The fawn soon ceased to flee.
Over her breasts my hands moved gently,
the new-formed girlhood she bared for me;
over all her body, the young skin bare,
I spilt my white force, just touching her yellow hair.

MARTIN ROBERTSON

APPENDIX IV

The Fortunes of the Poem

Semonides was included, together with Archilochus and Hipponax, in the canon of three leading iambographers drawn up by the great grammarian Aristarchus (*c.* 216–144 B.C.); but he seems to have made no very powerful impression on later Greek writers. The earliest author to quote him is Strabo in the first century B.C.; the other quotations, apart from those in the grammarians, come from writers of the second and third centuries A.D. The iambus against women, like fr. 1 and four others, owes its survival to its inclusion in the anthology of John Stobaeus, a Christian of the fifth century A.D., who drew upon existing collections.

The anthology of Stobaeus was not printed until 1535, when it was edited by V. Trincavelli. Conrad Gesner's improved edition followed in 1543, that of J. Oporinus in 1549; both of these included Latin translations. The first collection of poetry to include the iambi of our author was *Pindari et octo lyricorum carmina*, edited and published in 1560 by the great printer and scholar H. Stephanus. The poem about women was among those for which Latin versions were supplied by the Scottish scholar and poet George Buchanan; these were later reprinted in successive editions of Buchanan's works, and circulated widely. Stephanus confounded the iambographer with the lyric poet Simonides; and though Fulvius Ursinus pointed out the error as early as 1568, and several other scholars echoed his warning, it was to vitiate all editions of the poems until 1835.

The collections of the gnomic poets made by J. Hertelius (Basle, 1561–3) and C. Plantinus (Antwerp, 1564) and the collection of the tragic, comic, lyric and epigrammatic poets published at Geneva in 1614 included the poems, but did little to improve their text; but in the Latin version of the fragments of Greek poetry in Stobaeus which he published at Paris in 1623, Hugo Grotius effected notable corrections. The first English editor of the poems was Ralph Winterton in his *Poetae Minores Graeci* (Cambridge, 1635).

Like many other authors, Semonides had little done for him from the early seventeenth century until well into the eighteenth; then R.F.P. Brunck included the iambi in his *Analecta Graeca* of 1776 and again in his *Gnomici Poetae Graeci* of 1784. The real initiator of the great period of German scholarship is Christian

Appendix IV

Gottlob Heyne of Göttingen (1729–1812); and it was a pupil of Heyne, G. D. Koeler, who in 1781 published the only separate edition of the poem on women so far; he offered a valuable text and commentary. In 1823 J. F. Boissonade in his *Gnomici Poetae Graeci* and Thomas Gaisford in his *Poetae Graeci Minores* both edited the poems; both, like so many predecessors, confused the iambic with the lyric poet.

In 1835 the error was finally eradicated by Friedrich Gottlieb Welcker, who in *Rheinisches Museum* 3, 353 f. published a critical edition of the testimonia and fragments with an introductory essay that is even now invaluable. After Welcker the poems were edited by Theodor Bergk in the successive editions of the *Poetae Elegiaci et Iambographi* that form part of his *Poetae Lyrici Graeci*, which appeared between 1843 and 1882. During the nineteenth century the poems received much critical attention,[1] and the poems benefited from the studies of scholars like Gottfried Hermann (1772–1848), August Meineke (1790–1870), H. L. Ahrens (1809–1881) and F. G. Schneidewin (1810–1856). But some of the attention was over-critical; learned men tried to normalise the language, style and composition of the archaic author by emendation, deletion and transposition, not always with the happiest results. In a judicious article in *Hermes* 17, 1873, 327 f., Ludwig von Sybel resisted this tendency.

In modern times Semonides has been printed in the collections of Edmonds, Diehl, Adrados, D. A. Campbell and Gerber;[2] the two last offer a brief commentary, and Edmonds a maddeningly whimsical translation. The best text to appear so far is given by M. L. West, *Iambi et Elegi Graeci* II, 1970. There is a good English verse translation in Richmond Lattimore's *Greek Lyrics*, 1949, p. 8 f.

Paul Maas contributed an excellent concise article on Semonides to Pauly-Wissowa's Real-Encyclopädie III A, 1929, 184 f. The poem has been discussed in some detail and also translated by three leading modern German-speaking scholars. Walter Marg's small but important book *Der Charakter in der Sprache*

---

[1] For bibliography see W. Engelmann, *Bibliotheca Scriptorum Classicorum* I, 8th edn. revised by E. Preuss, 1880, pp. 668–9; R. Klussmann, *Bibliotheca Scriptorum Graecorum et Latinorum* I: *Scriptores Graeci* II, 1909, p. 280 f.

[2] J. M. Edmonds, *Elegy and Iambus* II, Loeb Classical Library, 1931; E. Diehl, *Anthologia Lyrica Graeca*, fasc. 3, 3rd edn. revised by R. Beutler, 1952; F. R. Adrados, *Liricos griegos: Elegiacos y yambografos* I, 1956; D. A. Campbell, *Greek Lyric Poetry: A Selection*, 1967; Douglas Gerber, *Euterpe*, 1970.

der frühgriechischen Dichtung (1st edn., 1938; 2nd edn., with addenda at the end, 1967)[3] contains an admirable discussion of and commentary upon the iambus about women. Marg's translation is in his *Griechische Lyrik*, 1964, 22 f. Ludwig Radermacher, *Weinen und Lachen*, 1947, 156 f. and Hermann Fränkel, *Dichtung und Philosophie des frühen Griechentums* (1st edn., 1951; 2nd end., 1962)[4] 232 f. have both translated part of the poem and have discussed it in a general way. Fränkel's treatment has the learning, intelligence and liveliness that mark all his writing, and it is helpful to have before me such an admirable statement of a point of view to which I am opposed. W. J. Verdenius, *Mnemosyne* 21, 1968, 132 f. (cf. ib., 22, 1969, 299 f.) gives a valuable commentary, which usefully supplements that of Marg.

[3] The first edition was reviewed by Hermann Fränkel, *American Journal of Philology* 60, 1939, 475 f. and by Hans Diller, *Gnomon* 15, 1939, 593 f. = *Kleine Schriften*, 1971, 101 f.

[4] The first edition was reviewed by K. Latte, *Göttingische Gelehrte Anzeigen* 207, 1955, 30 f. = *Kleine Schriften*, 1968, 713 f.

APPENDIX V

Addison on Semonides

That Addison had an excellent command of Latin is common knowledge; but Macaulay[1] was right in thinking that his Greek was much less good. While at Oxford Addison took the lead in a plan for a new translation of Herodotus, which Jacob Tonson was to publish.[2] Among the five persons who were to take part were Charles Boyle, later Earl of Cork and Orrery, and Dr. Richard Blackmore, afterwards Sir Richard; Boyle is known chiefly as having provoked Bentley in the controversy that led to the writing of the *Dissertation upon Phalaris* and Blackmore as the author of a vast epic on the House of Brunswick which has some claim to be the most boring poem written in the English language. Addison claimed to have translated one book, but to have lost the manuscript; in the end he backed out of the scheme; and it is hard to disagree with his biographer that 'he became aware that his scholarship would not enable him to work to the standards which he set for himself in Latin studies'.[3] Doubtless Addison had looked at the original; but he may have used a Latin version also.

The Spectator was designed to render learning polite and society decorous. It was addressed to women quite as much as to men. 'I shall take it for the greatest glory of my work,' wrote Steele, 'if among reasonable women this paper may furnish tea-table talk.' Yet in private Addison did not believe in the existence of reasonable women. In the opinion of his biographer[5] he 'thought women incapable of logic and not amenable to reason', and 'seemed to wish them all frumps, being apparently unaware of the qualities of wisdom to be found in the worldly members of the sex'. We must hope that his female readers accepted his assurance that the women known to the Greek poet were not refined, like the women of his own day; and we must hope that the formidable Countess of Warwick, whom Addison married a few years after the appearance of his presentation of Semonides, never happened upon that particular number of the periodical.

[1] 'His knowledge of Greek, though doubtless such as was, in his time, thought respectable was evidently less than that which many lads now carry away each year from Eton and Rugby.' This is from his essay on Addison, published in 1843.
[2] Addison mentions the subject in a letter to Tonson which is No. 1 (p. 1) in Walter Graham's *The Letters of Joseph Addison*, 1941. See Peter Smithers, *The Life of Joseph Addison*, 1954, 23–4.
[3] Op. cit., p. 24.   [4] Op. cit., pp. 204–5.   [5] Op. cit., p. 353.

Γυναικὸς ὃδὲ χρῆμ' ἀνὴρ ληίζεται
Ἐθλῆς ἄμεινον, ὃδὲ ῥίγιον κακῆς.

Simonides.

THERE are no Authors I am more pleaſed with, than thoſe who ſhew humane nature in a variety of views, and deſcribe the ſeveral ages of the world in their different manners. A Reader cannot be more rationally entertained, than by comparing the virtues and vices of his own times, with thoſe which prevailed in the times of his fore-fathers; and drawing a parallel in his mind between his own private character, and that of other perſons, whether of his own age, or of the ages that went before him. The contemplation of mankind under theſe changeable colours, is apt to ſhame us out of any particular vice, or animate us to any particular virtue; to make us pleaſed or diſpleaſed with our ſelves in the moſt proper points, to clear our minds of prejudice and prepoſſeſſion, and rectify that narrowneſs of temper which inclines us to think amiſs of thoſe who differ from our ſelves.

If we look into the manners of the moſt remote ages of the world, we diſcover humane nature in her ſimplicity; and the more we come downward towards our own times, may obſerve her hiding her ſelf in artifices and refinements, poliſhed inſenſibly out of her original plainneſs, and at length entirely loſt under form and ceremony, and (what we call) good breeding. Read the accounts of men and women as they are given us by the moſt ancient writers, both ſacred and prophane, and you would think you were reading the hiſtory of another ſpecies.

Among the writers of antiquity, there are none who inſtruct us more openly in the manners of their reſpective times in which they lived, than thoſe who have employed themſelves in ſatyr, under what dreſs ſoever it may appear; as there are no other Authors whoſe province it is to enter

ter

ter fo directly into the ways of men, and fet their mifcarriages in fo
ftrong a light.

Simonides, a Poet famous in his generation, is I think Author of the
oldeft Satyr that is now extant; and, as fome fay, of the firft that was
ever written.   This Poet flourifhed about four hundred years after the
fiege of *Troy*; and fhews, by his way of writing, the fimplicity, or ra-
ther coarfenefs, of the age in which he lived.   I have taken notice, in
my hundred and fixty firft Speculation, that the rule of obferving what
the *French* call the *Bienfeance*, in an allufion, has been found out of lat-
ter years; and that the ancients, provided there was a likenefs in their
fimilitudes, did not much trouble themfelves about the decency of the
comparifon.   The Satyrs or Iambicks of *Simonides*, with which I fhall
entertain my Readers in the prefent paper, are a remarkable inftance of
what I formerly advanced.   The fubject of this Satyr is Woman.   He
defcribes the fex in their feveral characters, which he derives to them
from a fanciful fuppofition raifed upon the doctrine of Præ-exiftence.
He tells us, That the Gods formed the Souls of women out of thofe
feeds and principles which compofe feveral kinds of animals and ele-
ments; and that their good or bad difpofitions arife in them according
as fuch and fuch feeds and principles predominate in their conftitutions.
I have tranflated the Author very faithfully, and if not word for word
(which our language would not bear) at leaft fo as to comprehend
every one of his fentiments, without adding any thing of my own.   I
have already apologized for this Author's want of delicacy, and muft
further premife, That the following Satyr affects only fome of the lower
part of the fex, and not thofe who have been refined by a polite educa-
tion, which was not fo common in the age of this Poet.

*In the beginning God made the Souls of womankind out of different
materials, and in a feparate ftate from their bodies.*

*The Souls of one kind of women were formed out of thofe ingredients
which compofe a Swine.   A woman of this make is a flut in her houfe,
and a glutton at her table.   She is uncleanly in her perfon, a flattern
in her drefs, and her family is no better than a dunghil.*

*A fecond fort of female Soul was formed out of the fame materials that
enter into the compofition of a Fox.   Such an one is what we call a nota-
ble difcerning woman, who has an infight into every thing, whether it be
good or bad.   In this fpecies of females there are fome virtuous and fome
vicious.*

Vᴏʟ. III.   A a   *A*

A third kind of women were made up of Canine particles. Thefe are what we commonly call Scolds, *who imitate the animals out of which they were taken, that are always bufy and barking, that fnarl at every one who comes in their way, and live in perpetual clamour.*

The fourth kind of women were made out of the earth. Thefe are your fluggards, who pafs away their time in indolence and ignorance, hover over the fire a whole winter, and apply themfelves with alacrity to no kind of bufinefs but eating.

The fifth fpecies of females were made out of the fea. Thefe are women of variable uneven tempers, fometimes all ftorm and tempeft, fometimes all calm and funfhine. The ftranger who fees one of thefe in her fmiles and fmoothnefs, would cry her up for a miracle of good humour; but on a fudden her looks and words are changed, fhe is nothing but fury and outrage, noife and hurricane.

The fixth fpecies were made up of the ingredients which compofe an afs, or a beaft of burden. Thefe are naturally exceeding flothful, but upon the husband's exerting his authority, will live upon hard fare, and do every thing to pleafe him. They are however far from being averfe to Venereal pleafure, and feldom refufe a male companion.

The cat furnifhed materials for a feventh fpecies of women, who are of a melancholy, froward, unamiable nature, and fo repugnant to the offers of love, that they fly in the face of their husband when he approaches them with conjugal endearments. This fpecies of women are likewife fubject to little thefts, cheats, and pilferings.

The Mare with a flowing mane, which was never broke to any fervile toil and labour, compofed an eighth fpecies of women. Thefe are they who have little regard for their husbands, who pafs away their time in dreffing, bathing, and perfuming; who throw their hair into the nicest curls, and trick it up with the fairest flowers and garlands. A woman of this fpecies is a very pretty thing for a ftranger to look upon, but very detrimental to the owner, unlefs it be a King or Prince who takes a fancy to fuch a toy.

The ninth fpecies of females were taken out of the Ape. Thefe are fuch as are both ugly and ill-natured, who have nothing beautiful in themfelves, and endeavour to detract from or ridicule every thing which appears fo in others.

The tenth and laft fpecies of women were made out of the Bee: and happy is the man who gets fuch an one for his wife. She is altogether faultlefs and unblameable; her family flourifhes and improves by her

good

good management. She loves her husband, and is beloved by him. She brings him a race of beautiful and virtuous children. She distinguishes her self among her sex. She is surrounded with graces. She never sits among the loose tribe of women, nor passes away her time with them in wanton discourses. She is full of virtue and prudence, and is the best wife that Jupiter *can bestow on man.*

I shall conclude these Iambicks with the motto of this paper, which is a fragment of the same Author: *A man cannot possess any thing that is better than a good woman, nor any thing that is worse than a bad one.*

As the Poet has shewn a great penetration in this diversity of female characters, he has avoided the fault which *Juvenal* and Monsieur *Boileau* are guilty of, the former in his sixth, and the other in his last Satyr, where they have endeavoured to expose the sex in general, without doing justice to the valuable part of it. Such levelling Satyrs are of no use to the world, and for this reason I have often wondered how the *French* Author above-mentioned, who was a man of exquisite judgment, and a lover of virtue, could think humane nature a proper subject for Satyr in another of his celebrated pieces, which is called *The Satyr upon Man.* What vice or frailty can a discourse correct, which censures the whole species alike, and endeavours to shew by some superficial strokes of wit, that brutes are the more excellent creatures of the two? A Satyr should expose nothing but what is corrigible, and make a due discrimination between those who are, and those who are not the proper objects of it.